Celebration 2000

CATCH THE MILLENNIUM BUG WITH ERIC AND

YOUNG WRITERS

DORSET

Edited by Simon Harwin

First published in Great Britain in 1999 by
YOUNG WRITERS
Remus House,
Coltsfoot Drive,
Woodston,
Peterborough, PE2 9JX
Telephone (01733) 890066

HB ISBN 0 75431 588 6
SB ISBN 0 75431 589 4

FOREWORD

Young Writers have produced poetry books in conjunction with schools for over eight years; providing a platform for talented young people to shine. This year, the Celebration 2000 collection of regional anthologies were developed with the millennium in mind.

With the nation taking stock of how far we have come, and reflecting on what we want to achieve in the future, our anthologies give a vivid insight into the thoughts and experiences of the younger generation.

We were once again impressed with the quality and attention to detail of every entry received and hope you will enjoy the poems we have decided to feature in *Celebration 2000 Dorset* for many years to come.

Contents

Upton Junior School

The Poems

THE FUTURE

What future is there for the young?
What songs are waiting to be sung?
As we fight and try to get peace,
Will wars begin to cease?
Why are we wasting Earth's power?
Why are we picking that rare flower?
What will happen to our Earth that is dying?
Will butterflies stop flying?
Will we stop poisoning the land and sea?
And will we stop cutting down trees?
Do Africans have enough to eat?
Will we stop eating a rare whale's meat?
Let's give Earth what it deserves,
And put endangered animals in nature reserves.

Donna Loveless (10)
All Saints Primary School

THE YEAR 2000

A new beginning
Putting an end
A year's just begun
Another just gone
Celebrate by partying
Or just simply lazing around.

People dancing, singing, laughing
Tears of happiness
Tears of sadness
Old and young all celebrate
So let's all have a big bash.

Lucy Parsons (11)
All Saints Primary School

The Third World

People not enough to eat,
Homeless children on the streets,
Empty tummies deep inside,
Travelling from mile to mile,
Just to get the water they need,
We have to help the sick and poor.

People not enough to eat,
Homeless children on the streets,
Flies hovering over their heads,
The villages are destroyed,
They have to evacuate their homes,
People captured and put to death.

People not enough to eat,
Homeless children on the streets,
Please God, help the Third World.
Stop cruelty to these people.

Mitchell Cox (11)
All Saints Primary School

Pollution

P eople chucking rubbish on the ground, all
O ver the environment waste lies rotting.
L iving animals struggle against man's excesses.
L ying on the water, bottles, cans, wrappers -
U ntidy, spoiling the landscape.
T ime and time again resources are wasted.
I gnorance and selfishness dominate
O ur world at the end of this century.
N ow is the time for change.

Emily-Jane Wheeldon (11)
All Saints Primary School

Celebration 2000

Celebrating the new year,
In five seconds flat.
Everyone's having fun
Shouting and screaming
The millennium is here
People serving champagne on a tray.

Wonder how they celebrated
The new year in the 17th Century?
Illnesses couldn't be cured
But they can now.
Archaeologists find ancient things,
It makes you wonder what life was
Like all those years ago.

What's going to happen in the future?
Will everything be run by computer?
Will the year 2001 be just as much fun as today?
What will I look like?
What will I be . . .?

Maria Zanelli (11)
All Saints Primary School

Celebration

The year 2000 coming soon, coming soon.
The Millennium Dome here to stay, here to stay.
All is well, thinking of the good parts but . . .
People are crying because children are dying.
Money badly spent, badly spent.
They could have stopped the crying, stopped the dying.
When the Dome has crumbled, Dome has crumbled,
Will we have learned by our mistakes, our mistakes?

Danielle Jackson (11)
All Saints Primary School

Celebration 2000

It's nearly the year 2000,
Hip hip hooray,
It's nearly the millennium. Yay!
Lots of parties and lots of fun,
I just can't wait until the millennium.
What new things will be built?
What if people can live on Mars?
It's only one more day to go,
Oh hurry up the year 2000's on its way.

Did you know that today it's actually the year 2000.
Charities have more money to buy more
Things for starvation and illnesses.
There's a new medicine that cures cancer
So not so many people die so young.

There are some things that I don't like about this
Millennium, like more pollution and loads of buildings.
But there are still nice little villages just like the one I live in now.

Natasha Dodge (10)
All Saints Primary School

Celebration 2000

It's the 31st of December
And there's a minute to go
Everyone is shouting and screaming
The tension is really rising
Three seconds to go
Three, two, one.
There's a massive roar
And everyone is happy
The millennium is here.
Everyone shouts,
'Let's celebrate the year 2000.'

Everyone shouts and screams with joy
They all start moving
Some to their houses, some to the pub
Some to hotels
While they're doing this they are chanting.
'Let's celebrate the year 2000,
Let's celebrate the year 2000,
Let's celebrate the year 2000.'

Richard Dyke (11)
All Saints Primary School

CELEBRATION 2000

People out late at night,
celebrating the millennium.
People talking, having a laugh,
partying, playing, having lots of fun.
What have we achieved?
Illnesses that can now be cured.
Starvation on its way out.
Men have discovered electricity so
people are not cold.
Schools now being built so children
can get an education.
This is all happening because
man is advancing, developing . . .
improving.
What can we expect in the new Millennium?
Cures for cancer, leukaemia?
Warring people stop fighting and talk?
Desperate people given a chance?
But that is for the next century
Now on December 31st we'll celebrate.

Emma Fairclough (10)
All Saints Primary School

CELEBRATION 2000

Let's celebrate the new year.
It's a new time, a new millennium.
We'll look forward to making people healthy.
Getting rid of cruelty to animals.
Trying to make it better for people.
Let's celebrate the last thousand years.
We'll look back at discovering medicines.
Discovering power, discovering new worlds.
Sending men up to the moon.

Let's celebrate two thousand years ago.
Jesus was born.
Trying to make God happy.
A tiny baby, God's son.

Victoria Dimond (10)
All Saints Primary School

MILLENNIUM

M is for music, laughter and celebration.
I is for ice, bobbing in people's glasses.
L is for laughter, jokes and fun.
L is for loving, caring and thoughtfulness.
E is for everyone having fun together.
N is for noise, loud games and parties.
N is for new hope for the world.
I is for interest and awareness and involvement.
U is for uncanny togetherness.
M is for millennium magic.

James Hayter (11)
All Saints Primary School

CELEBRATION 2000

The millennium is just around the corner
Hundreds of people celebrating
Jesus Christ being born.

Parties and discos everywhere, but where will it end?
Thousands of people celebrating
Jesus Christ being born.

Marking the changing seasons
Millions of people celebrating
Jesus Christ being born.

But think of all the people hungry and thirsty in poor countries
Billions of people celebrating
Jesus Christ being born.

Celebration 2000 is here!

Holli Bastable (10)
All Saints Primary School

CELEBRATION 2000

C heers! Here's to the end of the century.
E veryone is joining in the countdown.
L istening for the sound of Big Ben.
E xcited people all over the world.
B right faces enjoying the excitement.
R eally hoping for good things
A nd getting rid of the bad.
T errorists, bombers, bullies.
I nternationally banned.
O pen the new millennium
N ow!

James Axe (10)
All Saints Primary School

CELEBRATION 2000

C elebration's coming soon
E veryone getting ready for the big party
L ook around to see who's up past 12.00 am
E veryones' lights are gleaming
B oxes of chocolate for people
R ushing around to get food ready
A round the streets people getting drunk
T housands of people shopping around
I s it time
O r isn't it?
N ow, get ready for the big bangs, *bang, bang*
S houting and screaming, *'It's the year 2000. Happy New Year.'*

Sabrina Dennett-Lane (11)
All Saints Primary School

THE MILLENNIUM IS HERE

The year is 1999 AD,
The 12th month,
The 31st day.
The hour 11 pm,
The minute 59,
The second 59.
The clock strikes,
It is now 2000 AD
The millennium is here!

Peter Atkinson (10)
All Saints Primary School

2000 Revolutions

C alendar counting down.
E nd of the year coming around.
L ong year ahead.
E nd of year, start to think.
B ehave well, no world wars.
R ecycle all the bad things in us.
A new millennium about to spring.
T he evil people in our world need a fresh start.
I ngenius robots help us jump forward.
O n top of the world I'd feel if all these things came true.
N ow it's the day and everything's OK.
Let's make a better place of this world.

David Crewe (10)
All Saints Primary School

Celebration 2000

C elebrating a new year.
E nding the year 1999.
L oving the new toys you get.
E lder children stop bullying.
B abies start to walk.
R ooks are singing happily.
A luminium being used in factories.
T eachers not being stressed any more.
I magining what the next year will be like.
O ther people meeting new friends.
N ext year is going to be excellent.

Simon Lucas (9)
All Saints Primary School

MILLENNIUM

A new beginning,
A new year,
Celebrate with a pint of beer,
Lots of parties,
Lots of fun,
People shooting off shotguns!

The millennium,
The start,
Forget about old-age carts,
We've got balloons,
We've got decorations,
So let's join in the
Celebrations!

Katie Tizzard (10)
All Saints Primary School

STARVATION

S tarving people on the streets
T rying to keep alive
A lmost dying
R oaming people on the streets
V ying for attention
A ction must be made
T ry to help starving people survive
I ll people are dying, all
O ver the world. We must take action
N ow!

Luke Graham (9)
All Saints Primary School

Pollution

P eople listen
O bnoxious fumes, poisoned water.
L imited food supplies. Knee deep in rubbish.
L oud noise cruelty and hatred.
U ndo the damage.
T ry to conserve our world and each other.
I ncredible changes must be made.
O bserve the changes.
N ature will celebrate.

Steven Wheeldon (10)
All Saints Primary School

Millennium

At the disco,
We're celebrating,
Because millennium's waiting,
When the clock strikes twelve,
The millennium bug hits the computers,
They're going wild,
Everyone is laughing,
Dogs are barking,
Lights are shining,
We're having a party all through the night,
We're drinking some beer,
Music is playing,
We're dancing around,
We're eating lots of food,
We're going to have a barbecue.

Alec Payne (8)
Bransgore Primary School

Millennium Year

I'll celebrate with my friends,
With lots of yummy food,
Play lots of super games,
Then I'll have a barbecue,
With all my friends still here,
Now they have all gone home,
I said let's party next year,
I went to bed and woke up,
It's still millennium year.

Gemma Harris (7)
Bransgore Primary School

Celebration 2000

Food and drinks,
Lots of singing,
Lots of dancing,
Music running,
Loads of fun,
Balloons everywhere,
Banners up high,
Because it's the year 2000!

Natasha Daszykowski (8)
Bransgore Primary School

Celebration 2000

Everyone clapping,
Everyone dancing,
Everyone partying.

Robert Pidgley (8)
Bransgore Primary School

YEAR 2000

Fireworks banging,
Children at parties having fun,
Balloons popping,
Presents unwrapping,
Kids and adults dancing at discos,
Year 2000 has just begun.

James Cracknell (8)
Bransgore Primary School

YEAR 2000

Millennium night.
I am having a fantastic disco,
And some fireworks too.
Then open the presents as well,
And that is my millennium night.

Hayley Stapleton (8)
Bransgore Primary School

YEAR 2000

Fireworks, presents,
Kids and grown ups having fun,
Food and drinks, balloons.

Graham Boyes (8)
Bransgore Primary School

Celebration 2000 Disco

We are at the disco,
Let's party on down,
A barbecue out in the moonlight,
A bonfire with lots of sparks and fireworks,
We have lots of super games and lots of scrumptious foods and drinks.
I am going to open my presents now, lots of presents.
They have gone home,
It is the end of the party, it is over.
I can go to bed now, I will wake up and it is still millennium year.

Shannon Pope (8)
Bransgore Primary School

Millennium Celebration

The millennium celebration parties are here,
Hurry up we are waiting.
Hurry up!
Hurry up!
We want our Millennium Dome finished.

The year 2000 is nearly here.
The parties are starting.
So hurry up!
So hurry up!
We are waiting for the celebration.

So hurry up!
So hurry up!
We want celebrations to begin,
So we want to shout and cheer.

Stephanie Clark (9)
Chickerell CP School

The Millennium 2000

The millennium is coming soon,
Lots of things will change.
Planes will change,
Trains might change,
You could even order food.

The millennium is coming soon,
We could have holidays on the moon.
The swimming pools could be bigger,
And we could have invented a new digger.

The millennium is coming soon,
We will celebrate until two.
We will have a lot of things that are new.
The millennium is coming soon.

Craig Swann (8)
Chickerell CP School

The Millennium

The millennium will soon be here.
We are happy because it is a new year.
We peer out of our windows
It is a lovely day and we can't wait until
the millennium is here.
Many centuries ago it was different.
They didn't have cars or supermarkets
But the millennium is very near.
It will soon be here.

Leah Webber (9)
Chickerell CP School

The Millennium 2000 Century

The millennium is nearly here.
It is only a few months away.
Think back to the past.
Time has travelled very fast.
The Victorians had the cane.
It gave people so much pain.

The millennium is nearly here.
The months of February to December should fly past.
I bet I'll get another fishing net
And I hope for a super squirter.

The millennium is nearly here.
I can't wait to celebrate and have a party.
Cars might go very fast.
Cars were slow in the past.

Robert Rendell (8)
Chickerell CP School

The Millennium 2000

The millennium is here.
The millennium will finish.
People running madly
Every single day.
Up and down the stairway
Eating bread and pie and custard
And sleeping and snoring every day
And soon it will be the time to say,
Bye, bye Millennium!

Simone Rolls (8)
Chickerell CP School

MILLENNIUM SPECIAL

Solar panels by the ton
In 1900 we had none.
The weather's changing all the time,
It's really quite frankly on the line.
Millennium starts in 2001.
You never knew?
You never knew?
1999!
2000!
2001!
I really must insist we find somebody fast,
Or all this fun will never last.
The Millennium Bug is catching up,
With stronger power than a tiger pup.

Rachael Dodd (9)
Chickerell CP School

MILLENNIUM BUG?

M y heart is pounding,
I 'll surely faint,
L ights will go out, I can hardly wait!
L et's start the celebrations now!
E lectricity will be fine my mum says,
N ot true, I say,
N ot one little problem?
I s 2000 my date?
U nbelievably it's true,
M illennium is the word for me and you!

Jack Dinsey (9)
Chickerell CP School

The Millennium 2000

In the future the cars will be flying ones.
There will be moving floors and busy robots.
The boys and girls are playing with their rockets
And the children are looking forward to travelling to the moon.

The millennium is nearly here, the children are so excited.
The children are playing in the big wide fields.
All of the people are shopping for the great big party.
The town and country houses are going to have shields and alarms.
The children go to their new schools.
When the children go inside they will say, *'Hooray.'*
They will play in their very new school.
But if somebody goes out they will be brought back by the ray.

Adam Lister (8)
Chickerell CP School

The Millennium 2000

The millennium is near,
It's only one more year.
Busy people here and things happening everywhere.
Animals here and everywhere,
Children playing here and there and everywhere.
I could walk to school on my own
And talk on a digital phone.
I don't have to walk to a telephone.

We look ahead for the future,
In the sea is a new ugly creature.
I could buy a new house
And get a pet mouse.

Holly Gomm (9)
Chickerell CP School

The Millennium

The millennium is coming soon.
There will be parties and fireworks
And a whole bunch more (I expect).
The year 2000 is on its way, *whoopy!*
The millennium is coming soon.
Computers might do your schoolwork
Hi-fi systems might be as big as a wide screen telly.
There could even be four pound coins,
Triple glazed windows
And bigger wide screen tellies.
More chutes in swimming pools.
There could be new and faster trains.
Every house could be a mansion.
The millennium is coming soon
Machines might do all the work,
Have a happy year!

Jamie Shaw (9)
Chickerell CP School

The Millennium

The millennium is on its way,
Everyone can't wait till the big day.
The millennium is near,
I don't know why everyone's here.
The Victorians had the cane,
It gave people so much pain.
Think back in the past,
Sometimes we think very fast.
So many men are here,
No wonder there's no more beer.

Luke Silvester (8)
Chickerell CP School

MILLENNIUM CELEBRATIONS

Millennium celebrations are coming,
So I do want you here,
Can you do some sewing
And buy me a bottle of beer?

Come on, come on!
Come on, come on!
We want you here!

Louise Setterfield (8)
Chickerell CP School

THE DOME

The millennium is here, the builders are building.
The millennium is here.
In the air is a little bear who can't give me a scare.
The millennium is here.
The biggest dome on earth.
The year 2000.
The greatest year on earth.
The millennium is here.

Jamie McNair (8)
Chickerell CP School

THE MILLENNIUM

The millennium is nearly here,
Builders are building.
The millennium is nearly here.

The millennium is nearly here,
Children are flying with rocket boosters.
The millennium is nearly here.

The millennium is nearly here,
Cars are nearly here, taking to the air.
The millennium is nearly here.

The millennium is nearly here,
New food has been invented.
The millennium is nearly here.

Gareth Thomas (8)
Chickerell CP School

THE MILLENNIUM PARTY

The millennium is here now,
Let's get together and have a party.

The year 2000 is here,
It's time to shout and cheer.

Millennium, millennium
Come over here,
Because we need to shout
And cheer.

Jason Andrews (8)
Chickerell CP School

THE SOLAR MILLENNIUM

S o solar panels we have at last. They're saving energy very fast.
O h in 1900 what's a solar panel. It's better than a wet flannel.
L ook outside balloons by the ton, lots of fun for everyone.
A n event that's happening everywhere. Go outside, don't despair.
R ight on time in the glorious rhyme. Millennium special
right on time.

Christopher Le Pard (8)
Chickerell CP School

THE YEAR 2000

The millennium is near
It's only a year.
Busy people here,
Busy children there.
We look ahead to the future
In the sea a new ugly creature.

I could fly to space (in no time).
'When is millennium coming?' people say.
People talk and chatter.
It's only a year.
Animals here and everywhere.
I could walk to school on my own
And talk on a digital phone.
I don't have to walk to a telephone.

Laura Barrow (9)
Chickerell CP School

THE MILLENNIUM

The millennium is coming
The celebrations are here
The Dome is closer
The millennium
The millennium
Come over here
We need our year 2000
To shout and cheer
Come on, hurry up
Our year 2000 is here
It will be coming next year.

Oliver James Hibbs (8)
Chickerell CP School

The Day I Found A Pound

One day I found a pound,
It fell without a sound,
Out of a lady's pocket,
She was wearing a locket.

It fell onto the floor,
It was not there before,
She walked across the room
And then she heard a 'boom'.

She jumped into the air,
She'd had a frightful scare,
I put the pound away
And decided not to stay.

I walked along the aisle
And people did smile,
I walked into my den
And then wrote with my pen;

I found a pound!

Emma Hankins (8)
Haymoor Middle School

Wacky Opposites

As big as a house
As small as a plug in a sink
As happy as a child
As sad as a dad
As tired as a child gone to bed at 12 o'clock
As awake as a newborn fluffy chick.

Grace Benham (9)
Haymoor Middle School

BLUE

Blue is the colour of the sky,
How I love it way up high.

Blue is the colour of my eyes,
In them there are no hidden lies.

Blue is the colour of the sea,
Splishing, splashing, pushing me.

Blue is the colour of my best dress,
Mum will be cross if I get it in a mess.

Blue is the colour of Bluebell Wood,
I'd love to go there if I could.

Blue is the colour of Dad's cricket kit,
It should be white but the blue sock did it.

Blue is the colour of my grandad's car,
I wish he was here but he lives so far.

Blue is the colour I love to see,
Blue is the colour all around me.

Alison McBride (9)
Haymoor Middle School

SILLY OLD SIMON

Silly old Simon
went to Ireland
in a rubber ring
he came back
in a sack
and met a friend called Jack

Simon and Jack
had a chat
at a swimming pool
they both fell in
lost a ring
that's the end of Simon and Jack.

Rachel Hunt (10)
Haymoor Middle School

SERENGETI

Under the heat of the sun's burning rays,
The gazelle and the antelope slowly graze.
The lions and cheetahs sleep on a bed of sand,
While a shimmer of heat crosses the land.
The elephants bathe in the evaporating water,
The gentle mother with her wrinkly daughter,
Cleaning whilst having endless fun,
The large grey elephants under the sun.
As the long hot day draws to an end,
It's time to press up against a close friend,
The air is filled with sweet bird song,
Another day has been and gone.

Rebecca Marsh (11)
Haymoor Middle School

My Mum's Attempt To Decorate The Lavatory

My mum relies on the border,
To do all the work,
Relies on the border,
To hide all the mess,
On this occasion,
I must confess,
It did look quite bad,
Wacky and mad,
But when the border came along,
It hid it all.

My mum is not very good at bordering the top,
Around the light she gives herself an electric shock,
She could have caused herself to die,
You laugh so much you nearly cry,
Mum turns a shade of lily white,
It really is a funny sight,
There isn't any cheque, cash or fee,
To come and see,
My mum's attempt to decorate the lavatory.

But also . . .
We ran out of border,
We ran out of glue,
We ran out of paper,
Mum's broken the loo,
The paint brush is swimming,
In the lavatory,
So if you do want to come and see,
My mum's attempt to decorate for me,
You better come fast,
Her disasters might not last.

Natasha Maycock (10)
Haymoor Middle School

The Beach

The sand is smooth
The sea is calm
Some boys are playing football
Girls are jogging along
Dogs are chasing balls
There's a kite in the sky
A noise in the distance
The ferry goes by
We walk a bit further
The cars are all waiting
We stop for a while
To rest and look around
There are two boys fishing
Some are climbing the rocks
A jet-ski speeds past
The sun has gone in
The windsurfers pack
We slowly walk back to make
Our way home.

Thomas Angell (8)
Kingsleigh Junior School

Flying High

Here I am flying high
High up in the sky so high
Watching the birds as they fly by
Flying high, oh so high
As I watch the stars twinkle
As I say goodnight to the earth at night.

Danny Cunnah (9)
Kingsleigh Junior School

The Millennium

Celebrations, celebrations everywhere,
Celebrations, celebrations over there,
Celebrations up there, here and there.

Clock is ticking - tick tick ticking,
People waiting, excited and shaking,
Everyone is having fun.

Bells are ringing, people screaming,
Poppers popping, fireworks cracking,
Dancers dancing, everyone is having fun.

The millennium has come.

Zoe Shackleton (9)
Kingsleigh Junior School

A Bug

I saw a little bug
Crawling on the telly
Perhaps he likes to go outside
And eat a lot of jelly

I saw a little bug
Playing with a slug
Do you know any bugs
Who play with slugs?

A little beetle passed me by
Just like a tiny bus
Eating food
He made a fuss.

Joanna Langdown (9)
Kingsleigh Junior School

The Playground

The school playground is the place to be
Escape from your desk, your mind is free
Forget your books and pens for a while
But leave them in a nice neat pile
Grab your coat from your peg on the way
This has to be the best part of your day
Meet your friends and plan what to do
Play tag or football - it's up to you
Hope it doesn't start to rain today
Would just hate the weather to stop our play
Catch up on the news or talk about TV
Maybe invite your best mate around for tea
The bell rings and our play is at an end
Line up now - stand straight and don't bend
Back inside there's only two more lessons for today
Then - home sweet home - I'm on my way!

Elliott Perez (8)
Kingsleigh Junior School

Colours

The grass is green, the sky is blue
I am pink and so are you
The fence is brown, the earth is black
So is the colour of my cat

My sister's trousers are orange
My dad's are black and blue
My mum's are in the washing
The cat's got in there too.

Stuart Parkes (8)
Kingsleigh Junior School

DEVILS

Little Demon David
Was a spoilt brat

He had a little friend
Called Wayne
He is a right pain

At the end of the day
You are stressed
At the end of the day
You want a rest

I hide, I ride
But can't get away from him

At the end of my trip
I sighed, I cried
With happiness.

Alex Roff (9)
Kingsleigh Junior School

MUM

My poor mum,
is feeling glum,
because I said she had a big bum!

If this, she read,
I would be in bed,
so I've brought it into school instead!

It's not just her bum that makes her glum,
but when I poke her tum and call her Podge,
then I need to do a quick dodge!

Dean Lamb (9)
Kingsleigh Junior School

ANDREW

Artful Andrew jumping around,
He was never really on the ground.
This little gerbil met a cat who said,
'Aha, a tasty snack!'
But this little gerbil was not to be fooled,
He knew who did and did not rule!
So he faced the cat and with all his might,
He jumped in the air and began to fight!
The cat, of course, was fairly astonished,
To see a gerbil so very foolish!
Then Andrew bit the big cat's tail, who then,
Let out a mighty *wail!*
So Andrew retreated to his hole,
Pulling with him the cat's food bowl!

Oliver Benton (9)
Kingsleigh Junior School

SNEAKY SAMMY

Sneaky Sammy
The Prime Minister's K9,
Will, for any good, make a bee-line,
Newspapers, scrap,
Sugar paper and all;
He mushes them up,
With small bites
And when it's gone,
He takes paperwork.
It's a real pain
And then he starts again!

Jordan Trent (8)
Kingsleigh Junior School

HOLIDAYS

Holidays in the sun,
Holidays are always fun.
Holidays in the snow,
Is another way to go.

What I like best is to swim,
With the sea up to my chin.
Building castles in the sand,
Is fun on dry land.

Camping I've also done,
Tents in a field is great fun.
Boats on a lake and on sea,
Is happy for a family.

Skiing holidays are for the fit,
Wrap up warm take my tip.
Snow is white as can be,
Take care you could sink to your knees.

Pony trekking I've been told,
One has to be very bold!
To ride on horse back all the way,
Is what you do all day.

Mountain climbing, not for me!
I would rather climb a tree.
Climbing rocks might be fun,
If I was shown how it should be done.

To plan a holiday takes time,
We hope the sun will shine.
To win a holiday would be best,
I would really enjoy the rest.

Hope you will be happy,
Take your camera - be snappy.

Kerri-Beth Allen (9)
Kingsleigh Junior School

EXCUSES

I went to get the bus Miss
At half past eight
But I missed the bus Miss
And I ran to the school gate

I went to sit down Miss
But my chair wasn't there
I've ate a rotten apple Miss
Please get me a chair.

Alyson Warren (9)
Kingsleigh Junior School

THE MAN FROM PERU

There was a man from Peru
Who went for a ride on a kangaroo
It jumped so high
It reached the sky
And the man never said goodbye.

Michaela Roche (9)
Kingsleigh Junior School

Have I Got Everything I Need This Week?

Have I got everything I need this week?
Trainers
Socks
Book
Mobile phone
Diary
Trousers
Bag
Must forget
Smelly socks
Dirty underwear
Rotten apples
Or should I take my sun hat in case it's sunny?
I'd feel a bit weird
But never mind now, where are my car keys?

Elliott Trent (8)
Kingsleigh Junior School

National Poetry Day

National Poetry day
comes each year.
Brings everyone happiness
and a lot of cheer.
Poems everywhere
happy, sad or jolly.
Everyone's sucking a
poetry lolly.

Ashley Dwyer (8)
Kingsleigh Junior School

My Dog And Cat

I have a fluffy pet dog,
and a fluffy pet cat,
they fight for my cuddles,
and I don't like that.

I tell them to stop it,
or they won't get fed,
but then I feel guilty,
and we all curl up on my bed.

If I'm all alone and crying,
they'll cheer me up because I'm sad,
they rub round my legs lovingly,
when I have been bad.

We play in the garden,
with a bouncy ball,
have lots of fun together,
even if I fall.

I take my dog for walks,
down by the beach shore,
he splashes me with water,
and I love him even more.

Zoe Spiers (9)
Kingsleigh Junior School

A Winter's Day

All the leaves are brown and the sky is grey.
As I walk down the pathway I think of a summer's day,
So I could go out and play.

Clare Lody (8)
Kingsleigh Junior School

HEADMASTER

He scares the children,
The teachers too,
We all think
He's a silly old moo.

He smokes cigars in the toilet,
Smiling is forbidden,
He always gives you funny looks,
His smile is always hidden.

If you smudge your writing pen
Or make a small, small stain,
He puts you over his knee and . . .
Ooowww, oh the pain!

Rebecca Gillingham (8)
Kingsleigh Junior School

FUN

The winter snow, the summer sun,
The children outside having fun.
The waves in the sea crashing down,
The seashells that we all found.

We packed away our buckets and spades,
We found a cooler place in the shade.
Then we washed the dirt from our toes,
And Mummy said 'It's time to go.'

Jessica Higgins (8)
Kingsleigh Junior School

I Think

I think I saw a flying fish,
I think I saw a talking dish,
I'm sure I saw a mouse go *roar!*
I'm sure I saw a walking door.

I think I saw a teddy wink,
I think I saw a dolly blink,
I might have seen some running beans,
I might have seen a cat with jeans,
My mum thinks I made it all up,
But I'm sure I heard a singing cup!

Elena Vincent (9)
Kingsleigh Junior School

Growing Up

When you're first born you're as small as a kettle,
Your parents call you their little petal.
But when you're a little bit older,
You're as grumpy as a soldier,
But when you're much older,
You get much bolder.

Danny Hurst (9)
Kingsleigh Junior School

The Contergate

The world is sleeping
Whilst the Contergate is roaming
And there's no adoring when the Contergate is roaring

His claws need oiling
His toes are coiling
And there's no escape
When the Contergate is roaming

To him mankind are gingerbread men
Car wheels he sticks on a skyscraper
And hey presto, a lollipop

He's like a T-rex
He's a cannibal you see
He eats people like you and me

His breath is worse than burning rubber
When he runs the earth shudders
His feet are like rubber

It attacks its prey with a mighty leap!
He sneaks through the city with a creak
When he steps you'll go at least 10 feet in the air

The Contergate - what a name
Not just frightening, terrifying
His face the ugliest ever seen

How about a three course meal?
Me, you, a car
His tummy rumble, what a sound
Guaranteed to astound

The world is awake
Whilst the Contergate is asleep
And there's no solution when there's pollution.

Louis Robinson (7)
Pokesdown Primary School

My Cat

Cute face, a white line down her nose,
Tortoiseshell, the colour of her fur,
Cute paws like white socks,
Pointed ears, when you scream so loud,
Scared of next door's cat (Pickled Onion).
Hungry, miaowing at your feet every five minutes,
Comforting when you're crying or sad,
Sleepy, curled up in a ball,
Jumpy, pouncing at your heels,
Noisy, scratching at her kitchen cupboards,
Playful, chasing her tail,
Smelly, her food and biscuits.

Jessica Frost (9)
Pokesdown Primary School

MILLENNIUM

Now the millennium is near,
we are all going to cheer,
to say a great big thank you,
to the Lord's happy smile.
It is time to welcome the new,
and say farewell to the old,
for the millennium is here!

Hip, hip, hooray!

Amanda Dangerfield (9)
Pokesdown Primary School

AUTUMN LEAVES

It was a cold damp gloomy day
the lolly-looking trees sway and rustle their
orange leaves
they are trampled on by slippery people
who are sliding everywhere
the odour is obnoxious
the leaves are small, light and crisp
grungy and grubby
the wind blows leaves everywhere
birds fly south to find warmth
the leaves swirl in the wind
they are very colourful
hail falls from the sky, it looks miserable
naughty children play on the wet lawn
the sun is coming out, the lawn is drying
and hail is
flying.

Charlie McAlpine (9)
Port Regis Preparatory School

Circus Monkeys

From a hidden canopy a rope swoops down;
A clown pioneers up a wooden pole.
Screaming from the heights, a baby cries.
Suddenly a furry actor falls into a net of greenery.

A comedian chases another in fake anger.
Performers linger long on a highway of branches,
Whilst acrobats jump from twigway to branchway.

Dressed in brown like poor folk,
When their surroundings are boughs rich in greenery,
Hiding in the canopy waiting for the moment,
When they swing into the spotlight of the sun.

Alexander Brinkworth (9)
Port Regis Preparatory School

Mouse Workers

Grey workers
trying to be quick,
automatic packing
lickety split.

Scurry, scamper, scuttle,
collecting nuts and cheese;
pick up, put down,
storing for the freeeze.

Darting back and forth,
neat and careful stacking;
bustle, bolt and hustle,
nothing will be lacking.

Verity Macdonald (10)
Port Regis Preparatory School

AUTUMN BALLERINAS

Thousands of them,
All colours,
Swirling silently from the sky,
Lie down, still as can be.

Then up in
A jump, a sway,
The green audience is waving,
Their long green arms.

Suddenly all drop,
The show is over,
Until the wind,
Starts up again.

Alex Carless (10)
Port Regis Preparatory School

FIREWORK PARROTS

I burst into the sky
In a whoosh of colour,
Swooping high and low.

In a giant explosion,
I glide and whiz,
My feathers sparkle like a rainbow.

I screech as I fly
Like a green and red rocket,
And soar through the skies in a blast.

Rowena Newman (10)
Port Regis Preparatory School

Snowy Ballerinas

Like white ballerinas
Elegant as swans,
They float freely
Enchanting their audience.

Like white doves
They flutter down
Gracefully with light
Expressive movement.

Glittering frosty crystals
Glide down to earth
Landing so softly
In silent mounds of snow.

Every moment we savour
As the pretty snowflakes twirl,
For the prancing and dancing
Will soon disappear.

Bryony Gardiner (10)
Port Regis Preparatory School

Leafy Ballerinas

Leaves dance through air
        Like ballerinas spinning and twirling
They land on the solid ground, then blow,
        Scuttling like school pupils,
Pushing and shoving into a long line.

Hector Hughes (10)
Port Regis Preparatory School

Gerbils

A flat desert
of feathery sawdust . . .

Hardworking miners
tunnel further into it
using their shovels,
kicking debris back
in channels.
They smell danger ahead.
Soft noses start to twitch.
Nerves tense like toothbrushes.
The miners dive and scurry,
scuttling into burrows.

Not a sound or movement.

Max Cosby (10)
Port Regis Preparatory School

Sumo Wrestlers

Blundering along, these fierce great fighters,
Pot-bellied, overweight,
Thump
As the sweaty bodies hit the floor.
The opponent grinds his teeth
And the crowd roar.

The flat-footed heavyweight wrestlers
Finish their tiresome fight
Giving each other nasty looks
Away from the spotlight.

Alicia Lawson (9)
Port Regis Preparatory School

Aeroplane Birds

Flying,
Free in the skies
Like a glider,
The seagull soars.

A falcon
Stoops
Like a jet plane.

Like a cloud hovering,
A kestrel hangs in the sky.

The kingfisher swoops
Down like a World War
Bomber plane
To catch a fish.

Oliver Cripps (10)
Port Regis Preparatory School

Harry

He's a dull, overcast day with sunny spells forecast,
The murky green of the frog he watches,
If he were put in a large army base,
I expect he'd drive a tank.
If he were an animal,
He'd be a soothing silverback fish most of the time,
But at others a jumpy little cricket.
His hands would be permanently set at 9.00am.
As he catches his first fish of the glorious trip,
He's a small fishing rod, hauling up its catch.

Eleanor Ruddy (10)
Port Regis Preparatory School

Beavers

The busy building beavers,
down Winding Waters Lane,
cut down the trees and branches
to take to their wooden lodge.

The workmen are gnawing,
there is sawdust everywhere.
They are building huge dams
stopping the river's flow.

They are felling trees and carrying
wood with their spatula tails.
Then after the day is done
they relax themselves.

Alistair Larsson (9)
Port Regis Preparatory School

Mummy

A bent, motionless blade of grass,
Covered with dew,
Opening the morning happiness.

Warm milk
That heats your heart;
A small jug,
Pouring her love into you.

The early morning dove,
Sailing above you.
A delicate, cosy cottage.

Jack Bonham Cozens (11)
Port Regis Preparatory School

Lion King

The lion padded silently through the forest,
Watching his subjects at work.
The busy bees flying to and fro, storing nectar;
The graceful audience of grass,
Watching the beautiful leaf ballerinas,
Twirling their autumn tutus.
The sweet song of the bird choir
Lulls their audience of owls to sleep.

The great king stopped to watch the circus of monkeys
And their acrobatic tricks
As the mole miners worked round his royal paws.
Down by the river, the beavers build their dams,
To make pools of fresh water.
A water boatman glided across the lake
Using his oars masterfully.

Down in the land of the dandelion sun,
Is where the little insects run.
Small ant workers scurry all day
Finding grains of leaf and hay.
A concert of amateur violinists,
The grasshoppers and the crickets
Fight to attract the best mates.
The lion paces silently through the forest
As the squirrels work their nut factories
Cracking the shells and storing them for winter.

Lizzie Rabone (8)
Port Regis Preparatory School

AUTUMN

The smooth leaves are going to die in the cold season.
The leaves go brown.
The wind rustling the leaves.
The oak leaves go all mouldy.
The old trees crying because their clothes are dying.
The leaves begin to crumble and fade away.
The crispy golden leaves fall.
The squirrels collect nuts for the terrible winter.
The golf course's grass dying with hunger.
The bare trees shake with horror.
People get ready for Christmas.
The sloshy mud makes a soft comfy bed for the leaves.
The dark gloomy night rustling the trees.
The birds fly to the equator away from the winter.

Toby Murray (9)
Port Regis Preparatory School

DIVERS

A grebe dives to explore the weedy river,
A feathered Loch Ness monster,
Searching for silver,
Silver fish.
It darts into the cover of green wavy needles.
The colours flash as he dives.
Bubbles break on the calm surface,
As he rises to swallow shiny jewels.
Then the master fisherman dives.

Hugh Nicholson (10)
Port Regis Preparatory School

THE MAGIC BOX

My box is made out of solid gold.
With emeralds, rubies, diamonds and sapphires glinting in the sun.
I will open it with a silver key.
In my box I will put three stars
So when it is dark I will see my way.
I will put a sunny day in my box
So when it is cold I would take out my sunny day
So I will be warm.
I will put a dolphin in
So it will take me far away across the sea.
I will put a magic wand
So I can do magic spells.
I will put in a sword and shield
So I can fight my enemies.
That is what I will put in my box.

Edward Cripps (8)
Port Regis Preparatory School

FIREWORKS

They whizz and they bang
They zoom up and up.
The Catherine wheel screams as it
Scatters sparkly stars into space.
The bonfire glows like a giant torch
Just waiting for a pop or a bang.
The children scream as a firework roars
Around the sky pink, blue, red and gold.

Natasha Bell (10)
Port Regis Preparatory School

Autumn

The damp leaves fall to the soggy ground.
The bleak wind swirls round the cheerless trees.
The miserable day is grey and groaning.
Wet dark days make you tired and grumpy.
Squidgy grass to stop you playing
Games on the grass,
It sucks you up.
Big wet watery puddles right in the middle of the courtyard.
Yellow ochre, moth-eaten, organic leaves.
Gathering leaves outside the classroom.
Cold frost gathers on the soggy, dismal ground.
Little animals start to hibernate and squirrels collect nuts.
Howling winds make the trees bare.
The autumn sun comes out and blinds us.

Margaret Broadbent (10)
Port Regis Preparatory School

Autumn

The rich, glittering, yellow leaves sway to the ground.
The crackling crunch as the leaves strike the soft ground.
The sweet, smoky smell emerges from the leaves.
The sun creeps out from behind the clouds,
As the immaculate streaks of sun pierce through.
Flowers open to the colours of light,
And the birds sing at high pitch.
The light gleams on the grass making
Sparks before my eyes.

John Beloe (9)
Port Regis Preparatory School

DIVALI FIREWORKS

Sizzle, crackle, pencils shoot streams
Of fire
Zip, zap, plip, plap, butterflies dance and
Dip
Bombs boom, crick, crack and a big
Bang!
Fountains pour down like rain
Swispswispswisp
Rockets swish, swash, wish and wash
Up into the sky
Sshwitty, sshwitty, chuckries
Zoom
Fireworks are exploding
Everywhere
Pop, bang, boom and a loud
Crack
Zip, zap, buzz, zoom, off to the
Moon
Red, yellow, pink, green and
White
These are the colours of
Divali Night!

Kaushali Trivedi (10)
Port Regis Preparatory School

The Making Of A Kitchen

Take:
6 sharp cutting knives,
3 spiky stabbing forks,
10 smooth scooping spoons,
7 moulded round plates.

Mix:
14 plump old cooks.

Stir in:
Clanking heavy pots and pans.

Add some:
Extremely hot ovens and,
several wet sinks.

Beware:
The dirty cooks' trousers and,
sweaty red foreheads.

Finally place in:
A shiny steaming hot serving hatch
and enjoy
delicious food!

Jamie Inkster (10)
Port Regis Preparatory School

The Door

Go and open the door!
There could be a massive ship,
With gun turrets gleaming
And funnels steaming, or maybe a frigate or more.

Go and open the door!
Maybe there's a swift Spitfire
With wings shining
And the pilot trying
To shoot down a bomber or four.

Go and open the door!
Even if you're in the trenches,
With men dying
And men trying
To shoot down the foe with a roar,

Go and open the door!
Maybe there's peace,
Not war in the least!
Go and open the door.

Matthew Jonas (11)
Port Regis Preparatory School

Autumn

The leaves of autumn fall.
They crunch as you tread on them,
They blow from September to November.
The dewy grass of autumn sparkles in your eyes
As the cold, freezing grass of winter
Takes over autumn.

Harry Cutler (9)
Port Regis Preparatory School

EARTHQUAKE

A typical night in the city,
Quiet as ever, but,
A sudden roaring,
Loud and clear,
The city awakens,
Children are screaming,
A house collapses,
Glass windows shatter,
Telephone lines dead,
The fire strikes,
More trembling,
Paths and roads crack
Like potato crisps,
The trembling stops,
A crippled city waiting
for aftershocks.

Edward Leakey (10)
Port Regis Preparatory School

AUTUMN NIGHTS

The gloomy clouds make me want to go to sleep.
The golden, crispy leaves fall onto the ground.
The wind brushes my hair back.
All the animals hibernate.
The clouds are gloomy and grey.
The leaves sway from side to side.
The rabbits scamper quickly across the grass.
The round trees glitter in the sun.

Elspeth Meston (10)
Port Regis Preparatory School

THE MAKING OF A VOLCANO

To make a volcano you need,
One massive mountain with
A deep wide crater at the top,
A thick vent through the middle,
An enormous magma chamber within,
Tones of blood-red magma inside
And a long narrow side vent.
To create the eruption you need,
Red-hot lava pouring off the sides,
Ash blown everywhere,
Sulphurous heat invading the air,
Choking dark smoke forming a huge cloud,
Blinding stinking steam surrounds the mountain,
Explosive gas adds to the cloud,
Cracking rocks go everywhere,
You will have built a volcano
That is erupting!

William Van Hersten (10)
Port Regis Preparatory School

AUTUMN

It is a dark, dank day in the middle of autumn.
Trees swaying from side to side, to and fro, forward and back.
Leaves rustling in the wind.
Branches cracking in an autumn world.
An autumn world is a cold, wet world with leaves all around.
Young and old plants and mushrooms wilting and dying.
Leaves on the paths, plants on the grass
An autumn world full of hardly anything.

Thomas Dearden (10)
Port Regis Preparatory School

Autumn

The trees sway like drunks,
Clouds hover like onlooking civilians,
Felled branches corpses,
Green grass silent mourners.
The lawn-mower bulldozing
Civilisation,
Strikes terror into the heart of plants,
Young dandelion seeds run amok only
To be stamped on by playing children.
Mushrooms shading hot flies,
Animals in a deep deep sleep.
Now all is silent *sssshhhh* and go
Away!

Joshua White (10)
Port Regis Preparatory School

Goodbye Summer

No more hot weather to come.
Autumn is here.
The sun is struggling to break through.
The rivers and streams are rushing furiously
before they freeze.
The animals creep away to hibernate,
see you next spring.
The white grass shines like crystals.
The trees are slowly stripping their leaves
and showing off their bare branches.
Leaves dancing in the wind twist and twirl.

Emily Butler (10)
Port Regis Preparatory School

THE MAKING OF THE RAINBOW

Singing bright colours,
Dancing in the sky.
Shimmering, glistening shiny red,
Beats down on fluorescent orange,
Shivering, longing yellow
Sits just beside,
The twinkle of lime green.
Bubbling navy blue,
Leaks into sweating jeans of indigo,
Scaring mumbling violet.
Whilst dripping gloomy rain,
Falls from the misty clouds.
The sunshine peers out
As the rainbow sings in the sky,
Like a pack of skittles flying high!

Francesca Gulliver (9)
Port Regis Preparatory School

THE RAINBOW

To make a rainbow,
You will need to squeeze 90ml of blood out of a child.
Then cut up an orange very finely,
Fill a cup with some blazing hot sun,
Half fill a mug with some green slime.
Fill a basin with some shimmering blue sky,
Fry some violet flowers,
Mix it together,
And watch the rainbow appear.

Rupert Davis (9)
Port Regis Preparatory School

Monkey Puzzle

Collect the pieces,
Find his huge scary face,
Fit in his flaring eyes
And flapping ape-like ears,
Press in his small sweaty nose,
And curled sad mouth,
Make sure you clip in his small round belly,
That will soon shake like a bowl full of jelly,
Add to this hit nit-scratching arms
And some long thin legs as well,
As the puzzle begins to take shape,
What has appeared?

Louisa Fisher (10)
Port Regis Preparatory School

The Elephant

To make this quiet beautiful beast,
Shape cold grey clay into a crashing body,
Roll up tiny round toes,
Form huge flapping ears,
Squash on a short fluffy tail,
Mould thrashing sharp tusks,
Pound a huge chomping mouth,
Slap on thumping stretched legs,
Smash out a curling long trunk,
Punch in quivering, staring eyes,
Put it together and behold,
The elephant!

Michael Simpson (10)
Port Regis Preparatory School

To Make A Dormitory Take . . .

Four soothing empty beds,
With matrons scurrying about with sheets,
The flickering lights give a welcoming shine,
The musty door creaks with delight,
At the thought of the newcomers . . .
The sparkling ebony windows condensing in the cold,
The old polished mirror, so happy to be looked at.
Tied up curtains lovely and bright,
Colourful trunks start to emerge . . .
One by one the beds receive a duvet cover,
The sparkling beds are ready!
The assorted posters are varied in size,
The sound of drawers being stuffed with uniform,
It is now at full volume.
Suddenly every bed has a teddy,
All different in shape and size,
Creak, the door is open, grinning children all pile in,
The dormitory is alive!
Friends laughing,
Children shouting,
The fun day ends with the click of the light switch,
Everyone is content and one by one they fall asleep,
Listening to the click, click, click of the radiator.

Vaclav Borkovec (10)
Port Regis Preparatory School

MRS JAMES

She's a sunny, sunny day with a few spills
she's the holiday weather forecast
with a rainbow glowing beautifully in the middle.

She's a brightly painted cupboard
with tea collections inside,

and she gives off a scent of all fabulous things.

She's a pinky-white, a blossoming tree
bathed in light from the melted gold colourings
of the sun's rays high up in the sky.

She's a worn old thatched cottage with a blazing fire inside,

which attracts everyone's hearts.
A cuddly, treasured place, where everyone wants to be.

She's a friendly dog soft and small,
old and tired. But still loved by all.
An obedient, loving creature.

Put her in a field
and she would simply pick daisies and make the best of things,
and stay there till she was let free.

And she's skip out merry and jolly. Still young at heart.

Christina Nethercott (11)
Port Regis Preparatory School

THE MAKING OF A DREAM

Rushing noisy dorm mates calling,
The matron, furiously roaring,
Our talk is long, disgusting,
boring.

Bunk beds,
Glass-faced mirrors,
Flying, spooky, greyish duvets,
All these objects are quiet,
Not like,

Rushing, noisy dorm mates calling,
The matron, furiously roaring,
Our talk is long, disgusting,
boring!

Nowa Imasekha (9)
Port Regis Preparatory School

THE MAKING OF A RAINBOW

Take out your paintbox,
Mix your colours carefully,
Add continuous dancing rain
And beaming shining sun.
Then flick on a dab of sugar rose red,
Splatter on a blob of exciting luminous yellow,
Squirt on ferocious fluorescent orange,
Smudge in warm dazzling green,
Splurge about some misty sharp blue,
Shade in mysterious dark indigo,
Slip in some soft quiet violet,
But beware *the pot of gold!*

Charlotte Duncan (9)
Port Regis Preparatory School

The Blitz

The 2nd war was a tragic time
People died every second.
Hitler, a mad old man,
He went off his head
And then he shot himself.
Bombs fell, houses fell apart.
I don't know why people had to die.

England was defending herself,
But we did win the war.
We won the second,
So if there is another
We will win that.
I don't know why,
I don't know why
They had to fight.

Rollo Skinner (8)
Port Regis Preparatory School

The Making Of A Whale

Summon up from the deep,
Two huge flapping fins,
One slapping giant fluked tail,
Seventy rough scraping barnacles,
A big coat of thick blubber,
One large clotted blow-hole,
Two small blinking round eyes,
One humming beautiful high voice,
One snapping jaw of killer teeth
And millions of tiny helpless krill.

Richard Williams (9)
Port Regis Preparatory School

WHO LIVES IN THE CASTLE?

The stone steps are paved with gold.
But who steps on them?
Ivy trails from the old walls
But who trims them?
The tower tops of the gates are like wizards' hats.
But who shapes them?
The gardens are havens of rabbits and hares.
Away from the traps.
But who sets them?
The rooms are as tidy as can be.
But who tidies them?
Hunting dogs chained to stone walls.
But who chains them?
Birds swoop down to eat the food.
But who feeds them?
The spiral turrets are where it ends
But who lives here?
Me, of course, because . . .
I am the magician!

Alexander Bond (8)
Port Regis Preparatory School

THE DIPLOMAT

Dull and wet is this dreary fellow, like an ant.
Turn off his computer: he would become a newspaper,
The sludgy, dull, green pea-soup,
Waking at 5.30 to catch the train to work.
He'd be a very dull, gloomy grey if he'd be a colour.
The faceless concrete wall, kept busy like a computer.
He'd like to go down as a great politician.

Hugh Macpherson (11)
Port Regis Preparatory School

Alex

His sunny face looks so bright on a chilly autumn afternoon.
White, luminous phosphorescence frosting the grass,
A sleek, noiseless barn owl, soaring through the sky in search of
its prey.

He is so lazy, if he were a piece of furniture
He would be a comfy chair made of soft, velvety fabric.

An exotic, conspicuous boat is what he would be
If he were a structured construction.

Place him in a desert, and he would find some water
And play in it with a toy boat.
He's a huge plate of oysters, washed down with a glass of the
finest dry malt whisky.

Richard Rabone (11)
Port Regis Preparatory School

Adip

My friend is a cloudy day
With blue bits shining through the middle.
Dark purple like a gloomy evening
Put him in a forest and he would sit down and think.
He would not show any fear.
He is like a small smooth wooden chair
Next to a roaring fire.
He is a small tent with his feet sticking out the end.
He is a dolphin saving me when I'm drowning.
He is a warm cup of cocoa with a frothy bit at the top.
His hands are set at 6.45 because he is an early riser.

Kit Dorey (10)
Port Regis Preparatory School

The Battle Of Hastings

The Normans declared war on England.
They wanted land, it was 1066.
The Normans crossed the English Channel.
Halley's comet had been seen,
An omen, predicting victory.
The day at the hill was a dreadful time.
There was a great clash
The French at the top, the English at the bottom.
The French fired arrows down onto the English
As they ran up the hill.
At the end of the battle the French had won.
William claimed the throne
England was now French.

Max Hobbs (8)
Port Regis Preparatory School

Collectives

Curious box of creepy-crawlies,
Ocean of opera,
Legends of loneliness,
Love of lost people,
Erosion of eeriness,
Corpse of coldness.
Ticking of time,
Illness of tempers,
Voice of vanquishers,
Echoes of envy,
Sound of screams.

Shona Doran (11)
Port Regis Preparatory School

The Blitz

Every day, every night they waited.
Would they be next?
Bombs started raining from the noisy sky.
The planes flew up and down.
The searchlights searched the dark sky
To pinpoint the enemy planes
So that ack-ack guns could fire.
Children were sent away.
Crying, leaving their families
For safety in the country.
Sometimes to relatives
Sometimes to strangers.
When will they see them again?

Charlotte Peacock (8)
Port Regis Preparatory School

The Castle

What is lying behind the archway?
Nobody knows.
Nobody knows where its winding steps lead
Or what lies behind the misty mountains.
Nobody knows.

Shadows creep out from corner to corner,
And more steps lead down to the darkest depths,
Depths with creatures unknown to man,
Black witches' hats lie on the tall towers.
And crooked trees hang from clifftop peaks.

Alexander Pugh (8)
Port Regis Preparatory School

The False War

In 1939 all over England,
People were waiting,
Day and night,
Night and day,
Waiting for the bombing to begin.
Nothing came.
Then no-one carried the gas masks,
No-one put up their blackouts,
Then it came.
Bombs started to drop,
Evacuees were sent away,
Guns were fired.
The government thought rich people
Had too many foods.
Poor people only bread and milk,
So they started rationing,
That was more fair,
For all the people.

Isabella Good (8)
Port Regis Preparatory School

The Magic Box

My box has solid gold hinges and a little lock.
When you push the lid it opens.
I will put in a golden pebble because it sparkles like the sunshine.
I will put in a shining red ruby in the shape of a star.
I will put in a lamp with a genie to grant me wishes
And a little spaniel puppy with brown patches.

Adelaide Ruddy (8)
Port Regis Preparatory School

TITANIC

This poem is about the tragedy of Titanic . . .
There was a girl named Rose,
Who sat upon the Titanic and watched ahead,
She saw a white majestic shiny wall,
Closer, closer and closer they came,
And Rose saw it was an iceberg,
Closer, closer and closer they came,
Then, *ccccrrrraaaasssshhhh!*
Lifeboats dropped, full of people,
Screams and shouts were heard,
Echoing from every corner of the universe.
Then *split!* The great hull of the Titanic was doomed.
Rose jumped into the freezing ice-cold water,
Staring and staring at the horrible sight,
It looked like a pool of maggots,
There were so many people in the water,
Titanic was a night to remember.

John Hony (9)
Port Regis Preparatory School

SHAPES AND PATTERNS

A tree, like an outstretched hand, waving in the wind.
A snake, like a coloured piece of rope, sliding through
the long, wet grass.
A crocodile, like a log, floating on a gushing river.
An owl, like a fat fur ball, hooting like a car siren.
A crack in the ice, like a jagged edge of a knife.
A hedge, like a rock covered in moss, in a dark wood.
A bird, like a leaf, gliding down to the earth.

Alec Wayman (8)
Port Regis Preparatory School

The Blitz

All night and all day they waited for those
Magic words
'War is declared'!
So were they so magic after all?
Planes of all different shapes and sizes
Making all these horrible noises.
Innocent people lost their lives
While people cried and cried.
All night and all day people prayed and prayed
Would it be them or would it not?
Unfortunately some people weren't
As lucky as others.
Searchlights lit up the sky
While people tried to stop themselves from
Bursting into tears,
But luckily we won
And hopefully we won't go to war again.

Rosie Bell (8)
Port Regis Preparatory School

Moonbreaker

Five, four, three, two, one - *lift-off*
The first moonflight to take off
In a rocket, flying with shimmering metal
And a zooming lifeline following
Everyone was excited
Crash! It landed on the moon
Neil Armstrong was the first man
To put a foot on the moon.

Jake Dixon (9)
Port Regis Preparatory School

TITANIC

On the icy calm sea
Big and bold and strong
As big as a giant
Floated the Titanic.
Lights shining on the cold dark sea
Making splinters of light.
The four funnels silent and straight
Busily smoking away.
Sailing in the freezing sea
Sailing to New York
Would they make it?
Nobody knows.
People on board happy as could be,
Drinking, having parties, dancing . . .
Crreeekk crash!
Drinks spilt crowds running
To starboard and port
As the bow the big bold bow
Tips into the sea eight Eiffel towers deep
It seemed a pair of scissors
Cut the Titanic into half.
As she sinks to the bottom . . .
Silence! Silence! Silence!
Still calm, plunging to the bottom went the ship
The survivors in the lifeboats were crying,
Things and people lost.
1912 AD is a night to remember
The night the Titanic sank.

John Butler (7)
Port Regis Preparatory School

THE 2ND WORLD WAR

People waited day and night
To see if Germany would declare war
Was Hitler going to kill them or was he not?
People waited anxiously to see if the bombs would fall.
Suddenly there was a noise, it was a plane!

The plane dropped a bomb then *boom*!
The city flames.
Everyone panicked
Many people were dead
Was Germany going to invade England?

Sophie Hadfield (8)
Port Regis Preparatory School

THE MOON

As he lands on the moon
News flashes start immediately
People stare at the dark blurry
Pictures in amazement.
They are totally speechless.
They walk stumbling
Then they seem to get used to it quickly.
As they hop and jump around
Their air tanks were running out.
Just as they were going
They left a flag and went.

Matthew Carless (8)
Port Regis Preparatory School

An Anteater's Tale

In the forest tall,
I sat there small,
Munching on some ants.
I peered around, searching.
The gloomy mist is settling.
I stop my munching
And my vicious lunching.
I hear the monkey calling
And then he starts falling.
The birds are all chirping
And the jaguar is lurching.
The trees are always searching,
For the glorious light.
The sun is setting,
So I must say goodnight.

William Espensen (11)
St Andrew's Primary School, Weymouth

In The Rainforest

Creak, crack, the trees are swaying in the gushing wind,
Bellowing animals haunt the stuffy forest,
Slimy snakes slither, dodging trees on the forest floor.

Colourful plants are gleaming,
Trickling streams are hidden among the huge undergrowth,
Animals howling and growling,
Trees are growing, rivers are flowing,
In the rainforest.

Philip Winslow (11)
St Andrew's Primary School, Weymouth

If Only

If only they would stop building roads on hedgerows,
If only they would stop building houses on trees.

If only people put aluminium in bins,
I'm sure we'd have lots and lots more tins.

If only they would stop smoking cigarettes,
I am sure the ozone would have lots and lots less threats.

The litter I'm sure would feel a lot better
If we would just put it in bins.

The animals as well would feel much better,
If we didn't cut their trees and food down.

If only they would stop cutting down trees
And polluting the air with smoke and fumes.

Gemma Hunter (10)
St Andrew's Primary School, Weymouth

The Rainforest

Creepers creeping up and round,
Pulling the trees to the ground.
Trees swaying from side to side,
Making a place for animals to hide.
A slimy snake slithering low,
A tortoise is crawling very slow.
The colourful flowers are very bright,
They have only got a little light.
The leaves are different sizes and shapes,
Up above are monkeys and apes.
Everything lives in a different way,
The animals wish you would keep it that way.

Hayley Boone (10)
St Andrew's Primary School, Weymouth

THE SUNBEAM

Deep in the rainforest
The sunbeam creeps by
And softly touches, covering the land
The crispy green leaves
Turn to glimmering gold
As a toucan nips
At a crispy tip of a golden leaf
The parrots sparkle
With shimmering gold
And a chipmunk scampers by
Glimmering with golden specks
As the river flows silently by
It sparkles with golden shimmering gleams
Trunks of trees turn to gold
And shimmer and glitter, with sparkles
The humming bird sips
At the golden-petalled flowers
With its gold shining beak
Touched by the hand of the sunbeam.

Charlotte Dingle (9)
St Andrew's Primary School, Weymouth

IN THE RAINFOREST

In the rainforest the rain is trickling,
just like a child always bickering.

In the rainforest the birds are chirping,
just like a frog always burping.

Creepers climbing all slurpy and slimy,
also very slow and very, very grimy.

Paul Lawless (11)
St Andrew's Primary School, Weymouth

THAT DARK GLOOMY PLACE

As we enter that dark gloomy place,
We hear sounds of the animals race,
Can you see the cheetah in first place?
Maybe he is cheating.
Hear that dropping water drop,
Those towering trees tower up.
Animals
jumping
from branch
to branch.
It's a very
colourful
place.
Birds
chirping
very loudly.
The misty
forest has gone.

Lucy Chick (11)
St Andrew's Primary School, Weymouth

THE RAINFOREST

Down in the deep dark forest where no-one's ever been
There's a big fat rhino that no-one's ever seen
In the trees the birds are chirping,
Just like a parrot always gurgling
There's a funny sight to see
A chimpanzee looking at me
There's a giraffe amongst the trees,
Eating lots of banana leaves.

Rachel McWilliams (10)
St Andrew's Primary School, Weymouth

THE SUNRISE

As the sun comes up,
it sprinkles golden dust
upon golden hills.
My transparent curtains let the sunbeams shine in.
I wake up and I am blinded by the light.
I leap out of my bed, and look through my casement.
The sun leaps up from behind the hill.
Those sunflowers planted last year catch the glimmering light.
The soil like golden nuggets.
The rabbit cage glimmers in the light.
I run into my mum and dad's room saying,
'Look at the beautiful sun glistening in its pride.'
The tips of grass glimmering,
It's a beautiful sight in the morning.
The golden buzzard flying overhead,
The golden bee glimmering by sunlight.

The sun is a child giving sunkiss to
everything in its sight!

Amy Mowlam (10)
St Andrew's Primary School, Weymouth

THE FOREST

Enormous, gigantic, high trees
Creeping, stretching, swaying vines
Squealing, squawking, shouting animals
Misty, damp, stuffy forest
Weird, scary, moving shapes
Pretty, beautiful, colourful flowers
Swidgy, slimy, forest floor
Drooping, towering, massive leaves.

Lorna Whorlow (11)
St Andrew's Primary School, Weymouth

As The Enemy Came

The slippery rotting ground,
squelched all around,
As the enemy came,
in his nasty fame.

The birds squawked,
as the enemy walked.
Towards the trees,
trampling the leaves.

With his matches and his torch,
he started to scorch.
The animals scattered around,
then darted across the ground.

Sarah King (10)
St Andrew's Primary School, Weymouth

The Sun

Up in the morning,
Down in the night,
Mum why is the sun so bright?
The yellow ribbon wrapping the light green moor,
Dad my eyes are so sore.
Don't look at it for stream's a-glistening gold.
The sun created another world upon the golden dew,
A few people see it, some always do.
So that is it for another day,
What will come tomorrow we cannot say.

Luke Grant-Jones (9)
St Andrew's Primary School, Weymouth

GOLDEN EYE

The sun shimmers over the sparkling soft sea
dolphins jumping out of the soft, glistening sea
drops of the water falling like soft
gold nuggets. The soft, smooth calm sea,
sharks watching me with their golden
eyes. The golden mouths of the sharks,
they got shoved away with a
soft push. The sun shimmers
over the golden bridge,
shivering birds gliding
through the sky, rushing
from one island
to another golden
island. Golden
soft smooth
golden
shiny
red
blue
purple
turquoise cars
and golden
bridge.

Simon Dean (9)
St Andrew's Primary School, Weymouth

RAINFOREST HAIKU

Deadly animals
Creatures like spider and sloth
Rainforest is green.

Christopher Guarraci (9)
St Andrew's Primary School, Weymouth

The Golden Sun Rises

As the sun rises up into the golden sky
The golden flowers rise into the garden
Where tips of robins flitter in the sky.
The golden pond shimmering in the sunlight
As the reflection shines like
The pears and plums
Hanging from the golden tree,
As the blue waterfall turns to gold in the sunlight
And all the frogs hop into the golden pond.
A golden spider knits a very silky web
As a mouse with golden eyes tiptoes by.
Then the sun begins to fade and all
The things turn to silver in the moonlight.
But only until the golden sun comes up once again.

Rebecca Jerrard (10)
St Andrew's Primary School, Weymouth

Sunrise

A gold-tipped pond with a gleaming frog,
A shimmering gold butterfly,
The rocks glittered and gleamed with gold,
The green fish turn gold and glittery,
A dragonfly twisted and turned in his goldness,
Waterfalls run like ribbons of gold as the sun walks by,
The sun touches a grey dormouse, it suddenly glints with light,
A ginger cat sits watching the sun-touched fish,
A rose suddenly turns gold with the sun,
Then a squirrel darts past in a gold gleam.

Anna Otter (9)
St Andrew's Primary School, Weymouth

Gold In The Garden

As the sun does rise a little boy will awaken
and play his flute, and streaks of red, gold and orange
will flow.
He will touch everything with golden fingertips.
The dew will glimmer, the pond will shimmer.
The cherry trees will gleam with golden cherries,
the roses touching gold-tipped thorns.
A gold silent bee flies across the morning sun.
A golden spider spinning his web from morn till night.
Golden waves on a pond with golden lilies on gold
lily pads.
The tips of birds' wings glint in the morning sun.
A sunflower shines in the morning.

Abigail Almond (9)
St Andrew's Primary School, Weymouth

The Golden Sea

The golden sea, waves so high,
Sparkling seashells on the seashore,
The glittering shore up so high,
Shimmers like the sea,
The sea shimmers and shines,
Waves so high they touch the sky,
The sparkling seashells on the glittering beach,
The shore so quiet and still,
Children playing on the beach,
Crabs nipping your toes.

Kirsty Whelton (9)
St Andrew's Primary School, Weymouth

Gold In The Garden

A golden rose near the pond.
The pond a golden liquid.
The sun walking around the garden
Kissing or touching everything he sees.
Golden frogs born glistening.
Golden weeds glittering in the sun.
A newt swimming with a golden tail.
Dead frogs glimmering.
Gold fish swimming.
A golden seagull sparkling.
A golden washing line, golden clothes glitter.
Tall sunflowers swaying in the wind
With golden petals sparkling.
Drops of dew glimmering.
Dragonflies with golden wings
Sparkling in the sunlight.
Golden footprints.

Becky Jones (9)
St Andrew's Primary School, Weymouth

The Golden Sun's In The Garden

The sun was dazzling,
Glistening on the golden tree
With the golden bee.
The golden flies in the golden sky.
The sun twinkled on the cat's eye,
Like a star in the sky.
The golden mole in a golden hole.

Sophie Herbert (10)
St Andrew's Primary School, Weymouth

A Rainforest Haiku

Green slithering snake
flies from swaying trees in the wind
landing is superb.

Coloured things all around
vivid butterfly flitters
floats on a flower.

Hairy spider creeps
injects poison in things, kills
animals dying.

Rainforest is hot,
steamy, rains every day,
different animals.

Trees swaying in breeze
and over fifty feet tall,
standing like soldiers.

Amie Passoni (9)
St Andrew's Primary School, Weymouth

The Golden Day

The gold ladder to the pool
Liquid, gleaming bright as a gold star
The tiles, sparkling and shimmering.
The dew on the grass weaved in and out
Like a spider's web.
In the field beside, there were thousands of
buttercups, as gold as can be.

Beckie Chorley (9)
St Andrew's Primary School, Weymouth

RACING CARS

Start your engines
Vroom! Vroom!
Get set *Go!*
Vroooooom! Vroooooom!
They're off
Number one coming to a corner
Screeeeeeech!
He's skidded and gone into the barrier
Whoosh!
He's gone up in flames
Neenor! Neenor!
Here comes an ambulance
Number three in the lead now
Vroom!
Number eight, superb overtaking there
The man's been taken into the ambulance.
Coming up to the finish line
Number three and number eight
Wheel to wheel.
Vroooooooooom!
Number three's won
Hurray!
He's won the cup.

Matthew Taylor (8)
St Andrew's Primary School, Weymouth

CAT HAIKU

Shadow moving slow
lies down, claws slide into paws
falls asleep on chair.

Jack Bennett (9)
St Andrew's Primary School, Weymouth

THE GOLDEN SUN

Slowly but quietly now, the sun as
She walks into her dark gloomy cave,
She touches a waterfall and stream of black;
And in a flash, the waterfall and stream
Turn into a sparkling, golden liquid,
Shimmering gold fish jumping up and down,
In and out of the water,
Their fins flash like golden lightning;
She walks over golden corn,
She comes to three trees,
Apple, pear and banana,
Touches each in turn
With her golden rays,
Golden apples!
Golden pears!
Golden bananas!
Then suddenly a golden bell starts to ring.
She runs through the golden corn,
Runs to her home and closes the door;
It's dark now.

April Hyde (9)
St Andrew's Primary School, Weymouth

GOLDEN SUN

Golden leaves on golden trees.
Sparkles of gold on monkeys.
Snake, sliding for its prey and it has spots of gold on its back.
A parrot, flying in the air over the trees and the glitter from the sun.
A waterfall of gold.
A stream turned to gold like magic.

Samantha Tugwell (9)
St Andrew's Primary School, Weymouth

Gold

The sun has risen from the night
The golden rays hit my red desk and turn it to pure gold
The golden beams smash my mirror to gold
The TV blew up with golden light
The door blazed with golden fiery light
The hamster cage shimmered with gold
So did the hamster
My books spattered with gold
My football boots glowed with golden sparks
My sweets flashed into golden nuggets
My floor exploded into gold like a bomb
My roller blades glinted and sparkled with gold
Everything was gold, gold, gold
Gold, a flash of gold, a glint of golden light
Gold swirling around my head
Gold!

Simon Briant (9)
St Andrew's Primary School, Weymouth

The Sun And The Moon

The moon goes down and the sun comes up.
The flowers open and they sparkle.
The animals awake and they crawl around.
The fish swim around and around in the glinting pond.
A trickling stream joins a big river.
The flowers shut.
The animals go to bed.
The fish stop swimming
And the river dies down.
The moon comes up and the sun goes down.

Digby Gill (9)
St Andrew's Primary School, Weymouth

The Rainforest

The sun comes up and sprays
The rainforest in gold.
She walks on the grass,
Turning it to gold.
The birds that fly by,
Change to gold as if by magic.
Frog jumps through the glistening leaves,
That fall from the trees.
Where ginger orang-utans leap!
Snakes slither and slide,
Searching for snacks.
The sun sees the tiny birds
Trying to fly from their nests.
Golden butterflies, fluttering past sloths,
Crawling slowly and carefully
In the golden rainforest.

Olivia Clyne (9)
St Andrew's Primary School, Weymouth

Yellow Is My Favourite

Yellow is my favourite,
like a marshmallow.
The sunlight shining on the windows
waking you up while you hear
the rooster go 'Cluck, cluck, cluck.'
The colour of his eggs are yellow,
so soft as they lay in the light
which is burning, burning ever so bright.

Hannah Day (8)
St Andrew's Primary School, Weymouth

Gold

As the sun rises high,
the little cocker spaniel
wakes up and chases
a butterfly.
A bee goes past,
so the dog goes after the bee.
In a field down the road
a horse rolls in the mud.
But the dog fell in
a pond and now he is
glittering.
The pony, covered in
golden mud on his
golden back.

Cora Newman (9)
St Andrew's Primary School, Weymouth

Golden World

The sun says his last word to the golden world.
He says 'Goodbye' to the gold things like
The shimmering streams running down the banks
And the gold sparkles on the rooftops,
Gleams on the golden fields with the gold cows
And shines on the mountains
And shines through the windows of cars.
People moving in the golden road.
Golden droplets fall down on people
And golden wings in the golden sky
And near the sea is the horizon
And then the sun goes down
And comes back up in silver.

Louisa Kennedy (9)
St Andrew's Primary School, Weymouth

THE GOLDEN RAYS

A peak of golden rays,
Over the bumpy hills.
As it swerves nearer,
The sunlight kills.
The silver moonlight struck upon the moor.
The golden sunrays bounce,
Until it's striking my door.
The sunrays hit the soft, silver mane
Of a beautiful, silver horse.
The rays carry on,
On its easy course.
The sunrays are still bouncing,
And it's nearly the end of the day,
The sunrays start to rot,
Then they start to decay.

Luke Perkins (9)
St Andrew's Primary School, Weymouth

THE FALLING IRON MAN

The Iron Man is falling,
Clang, clang, clonk.
He is falling off a cliff
with a *clink, clonk, clonk.*
But where will he end up?
All his bits coming off
falling off a cliff he is.

Acrrraaaassssh
Lying on the beach, he has
shattered into pieces
No more tractors being bitten off.

Magdalena Rowling (9)
St Andrew's Primary School, Weymouth

GLINTS

Glints, glints, flashing glints glow all glints.
Glints flash, glints thrash of glimmering gold.
I've got a goldfish called Glints, who sparks
In the sun all day
With glittering gold I say
Glints, glints, sparkling glints are all like gold.
They run around the garden like a big, fat toad.
Glints, glints, glowing glints glow like gold.
They glow all day in the garden shed
They make it all to gold.
They sparkle, they gleam with shimmering gold.
They make the house glint.
Glints, glints, streaming glints
Make the flower too gold.
Glints, glints, dull glints
Flash all like gold.
They make the garden look awfully dull
So they don't make anything gleam.

Jack Aston (10)
St Andrew's Primary School, Weymouth

IRON MAN POETRY

Crang, clank, clong, crash
Trang, rattle, boom, smash.
Scrape, creak, wallop, plink,
Chime, clatter, boof, tink.
Crong, ctank, crash, crash,
Then there was a big, big smash.
The iron man was
Falling down the cliff!

Natasha Mann (8)
St Andrew's Primary School, Weymouth

GOLD

As the shimmering sun
Rose up from out of the sky,
A golden, glimmering woman
With a golden, glistening cloak,
Golden boots and golden hair,
Swung around smoothly.

As the golden, glimmering woman
Slowly touched the bees
With her golden hands,
The bees quickly turned to gold.
She shone down on their wings,
Glistening in the sun.

A dragonfly flew across her face
She reached out her shimmering arm
And gently touched the dragonfly.
It turned to gold,
Smoothly flapped its wings
In broad daylight.

She touched frogs in the pond,
Suddenly they turned to gold.
She touched the reeds into gold
They glistened in the sun
As the woman slowly moved,
Her golden cloak shone
And glimmered too.

Jordan Buckley (9)
St Andrew's Primary School, Weymouth

Clish-Clash

The Iron Man
Falling down a cliff
Crash!

Bits falling
Bits breaking
Boom! Boom! Ting!

Clonk! Clang!
Twang!
The sound of shattering
Body and bits, like arms,
Legs, body and a head
As big as a bed and then
Silence!

Jessica Ellis (9)
St Andrew's Primary School, Weymouth

Crash, Wallop

Crash, wallop goes the monster.
Down the cliff goes the Iron Man
Off goes his head, then his arms.
Clang, crash, smash goes the monster.
Then his legs fall off,
Dragging the feet behind them.

Clunk, clank like a rusty old train,
Smash, all the bolts have gone.
And *crash*, shattered in pieces
All over the beach,
Swallowed up by the sea.

Oliver Pankhurst (8)
St Andrew's Primary School, Weymouth

Clinkety-Clink

Clinkety-clink,
Clinkety-clank,
Down the cliff, like a tank
Goes the Iron Man.
He bumps here,
He bumps there,
He just bumps everywhere.
The Iron Man's legs bobble off,
Arms, eyes and everything,
He scatters over boulders, rocks,
Over trees.
No more Iron Man.
Everything has gone quiet.

Lewis Ironside (8)
St Andrew's Primary School, Weymouth

Red

Red is the sunshine
Bright, bright red.

Red is your face
When you are angry.

Red is the fire
In the night-time.

Red is the blood
When your finger
Is bleeding.

Red are the bricks
On the houses.

Jack Godwin (9)
St Andrew's Primary School, Weymouth

The Iron Man Disaster

The ping of an eye
a clang of a head
the sound, as heavy as some lead.

The creaking of a leg,
the scratching of an arm,
maybe he'll land on top of a farm.

A twang of a finger,
a boof of a ear,
oh what a lot of fear.

A clonk of a body,
oh what a sound
will he every be found?

There the Iron Man lay
he did not know the day
silence!

David West (8)
St Andrew's Primary School, Weymouth

Gone!

Clash, clang falls the Iron Man.
As his arm flew away.
Bouncing down the rocks.
His head went bong,
His legs went bashing
All the way down the cliff.

Stacy Hickman (9)
St Andrew's Primary School, Weymouth

TING, TANG, CRASH

On the cliff the Iron Man stares,
A wobble, a tobble,
Crash!
Bits and bobs clink, clank,
Rumble, tumble
Arms, legs, clitter, clatter everywhere
Rumble, tumble everywhere.

Clink, clank, creak, wang,
Ping, plink, plink, ping
Smash!
Ting, ting, ting.
Stop! It's peaceful
Tink, tink, tink, tink, tink, tink, tink . . . *smash.*

Robyn Acutt (9)
St Andrew's Primary School, Weymouth

CRASH CRASH GOES THE METAL

Crash, crash, clank, clank,
bang, bang, ping, pong.
The Iron man falls
Crash, bang, wallop, pang
ting, ping, pang, twang, bang
falls the Iron Man, bang!
Crash, wallop, ping, ping.

Mark Lund (8)
St Andrew's Primary School, Weymouth

Could This Be The End Of The Iron Man?

Slowly working his way towards the cliff
when suddenly the ground from underneath the Iron Man
seemed to disappear, crash, plonk, thwack.
What a noise, clink, tonk, prink, cronk as the Iron Man
brushed against the rocks. Legs flying off, screws popping out,
his head crashing to the ground.
His eyes bouncing on the ground when . . .
Caboom!
The Iron Man shattered into pieces and then
all you could hear was the whistling of the wind
and the rushing of the waves.

Jenny Greenhalgh (9)
St Andrew's Primary School, Weymouth

Iron Man, Going, Going, Gone

Clink, clang, down the cliff,
Bashing down went the Iron Man.
Booming down on the rocks
Crashing down on the ground.
His hand, like a crab on its back.
His head, all rusted, clanged down the cliff.
His eyes popped out,
His arms fell off
And his body was all in pieces.

Neah White (9)
St Andrew's Primary School, Weymouth

Gone!

Crash, crash, crash!
Booming, booming, booming,
Crash, crash went the Iron Man.
Clink, bang, where's the Iron Man's arm?
Where is his head?
His head was rusty,
His leg went dusty.

David John Day (9)
St Andrew's Primary School, Weymouth

The Fall Of The Iron Man

Crash, bang, wallop
Went the Iron Man.
His arms fell off, clank.
His head sounded like an earthquake.
His eyes went plink, plink.
His legs clanged on rocks.
Bits of him everywhere.

Jamie Russell (9)
St Andrew's Primary School, Weymouth

Fireworks

Fireworks are shooting stars,
they are colourful and flashing.
They are green and blue,
they bang and boom!
They whoosh up into the sky,
the cartwheels go round
and round and round.

Harry McWilliams (8)
St Andrew's Primary School, Weymouth

The Iron Man's Crash

Crash, bang, plink, plonk,
Went the Iron Man.
His arm broke off.
His dustbin head clanked
Into the dark, blue sea.
Down the cliff he went,
Legs going everywhere.
All was still, all was still.

Kathryn Fisher (9)
St Andrew's Primary School, Weymouth

Crash, Smash

The Iron Man is falling down the cliff
Crashing, dashing, down comes the leg.
Clonk, plonk, down comes the head as big as a bed.
Clang, clank, down comes the hand.
Booming, rattling comes his arm.
Rattling comes his body and a clink.
Suddenly, silence.

Sadie Roberts (9)
St Andrew's Primary School, Weymouth

Barn Owls

White, soft barn owl, hooting in the night.
Glimpsing. glimpsing, spying for its prey.
Crash, bang, wallop, at last he's found his prey.
He soared through the sky,
Back down to his nest.
Where his children and wife were waiting.

Natalie King (8)
St Andrew's Primary School, Weymouth

It's Amazing!

Isn't it amazing how fax machines can send messages miles away?
Isn't it amazing how you can contact people miles away with a phone?
Isn't it incredible how a computer can play sounds?
Isn't it wonderful how a TV can show programs all over the country?
Isn't it wonderful how a radio can play the same song all over
the world?
Isn't it amazing?

Hal Barker (9)
St Andrew's Primary School, Weymouth

Sea

The sea is an amazing, wonderful place,
It is blue and shiny all over.
The sea is where the boats sail and fish swim.
The sea is where the dolphins and whales live.
The sea is where the small children play in the day.
The sea is where the children throw stones and rocks,
But most of the all, the sea is a wonderful, amazing place.

Tamara Collier (8)
St Andrew's Primary School, Weymouth

Barn Owls

At night the barn owls are swooping, staring out of the sky,
gliding through the darkness.
Soaring, gliding, swooping back into their homes,
but not for long.
They were back out, staring, gliding, soaring, swooping,
gliding all over the place.
Their feathers are soft and gold.

Jemma Tewkesbury (8)
St Andrew's Primary School, Weymouth

2000 (Millennium Bug)

Black bug, gloomy bug, dark bug.
Crashes on the computer.
Crashes on the TV.
Crashes on the music systems.
This little thing is creeping around.
No one knows where it is.
So get your spray out.
Start spraying here and there.
You've got to get your spray out quickly.
Go! Go! Go!

Adam Hillier (8)
St Andrew's Primary School, Weymouth

Green

Green is the colour of the wavy grass, blowing from
side to side in the wind.
Green is the colour of grassy hills outside my front door.
Green is the colour of juicy apples when I take a bite
my mouth lights up.
Green is the colour of leaves on the top of trees.
Green is the colour of the stems holding up all the
beautiful flowers in your garden.
Green is the colour of seaweed under the sea.

Cassie Hall (8)
St Andrew's Primary School, Weymouth

My Bed

As I snuggle right down
in my warm, cosy bed.
I close my brown eyes
and put down my head.

I see in my dreams
a brand new bike
So I can ride up the hills
and I don't have to hike.

Soft and fluffy,
cosy and warm.
I sleep in my bed
until the crack of dawn.

Amy Nicholls (8)
St Andrew's Primary School, Weymouth

Colours

Colours are lovely, like blue, yellow, red, orange, green.
Colours are horrible, like purple, black, brown.
I like beautiful colours.
These are bright colours, yellow, orange.
These are dark colours, black, brown, purple.
These are normal colours, red, blue, green.
My favourite colour - blue
These are nice colours, red, yellow, blue, orange, green.
These are horrible colours, purple, black, brown.

Amy Chick (8)
St Andrew's Primary School, Weymouth

The Zoo

Giraffes are tall and have long necks to reach
the leaves in the trees and bend over to the grass.
Monkeys swinging tree to tree and tails that
help them to balance and grip.
Elephants are big, fat and round, with big trunks
that sniff on the ground.
Parrots squawking in the cage and making
rude noises.

Thomas Mereweather (8)
St Andrew's Primary School, Weymouth

Monkeys

Monkeys are intelligent,
They live high in the treetops,
They feed on fruit and insects.
Some monkeys feed on animals,
They swing through the trees like gymnasts.
I wish I was a monkey.

Charlie Gray (8)
St Andrew's Primary School, Weymouth

Cheetah

Cheetah, cheetah, at such speed.
Why do you cheat in every race?
Is it because of your name
Or because you want to win?
Anyway, you always win!

Charlie Randall (8)
St Andrew's Primary School, Weymouth

My Friend, Fluffy Fat Cat

My friend, Fluffy Fat Cat, sits on a massive mat.
He wears a cool cap,
His best animal is a bat and his name is Pat!
One day he walked across the road and splat!
That was the end of my friend Fluffy Fat Cat.
I bought another cat,
He did not wear a cool cap,
He did not sit on a massive mat,
His best animal was not a bat
And his name is not Pat, it's Tat!

Roseanne Rogers (8)
St Andrew's Primary School, Weymouth

Rainforest

Parrots, squawking
Monkeys, chattering
Butterflies, fluttering
Spiders, crawling
Ants, scuttling
Leaves, falling
Trees, swaying
Birds, singing
This is a rainforest!

Joseph Butcher (8)
St Andrew's Primary School, Weymouth

THE BLUE WHALE

The sea is rough, the sky is clear,
among the waves, the whales appear.
Jumping and swimming with just one wish
to find and eat lots of fish.
The ships and boats are passing near
the whales dive down to hide with fear.
Then up again to start their playing
from their spouts the water's spraying.
For whales to live, we must behave
not to kill, but love and save!

Steven Rockett (8)
St Andrew's Primary School, Weymouth

RAINFOREST

The rainforests have millions of trees
Billions of leaves blowing in the breeze
But here come the saws
How the birds caw
Ugh! The birds fear
The saws are near
Soon there will be thousands of roads
Instead of trees.

Stacey Vanstone (8)
St Andrew's Primary School, Weymouth

THE MATCH

On the day before the match
When I go to sleep
All I can think about
Is the ball at my feet.

I dream about my kit,
The top, the shorts, the socks,
And my boots
Are all a perfect fit.

We start the game,
We run like mad,
They have a shot
But it's really bad.

The goalie throws it to me
I control it on my knee
A twist and swivel,
A fast dribble.
Into space is where I want to get
My left foot shoots
The ball is in the net.

One - nil and we've won,
And someone calls my name
Then I wake up
It's only Mum!

Thomas Flynn (7)
St Thomas Garnet's School, Bournemouth

MY FAVOURITE SPORT

I love all kinds of different sports,
But football is the best.
I love to run and kick the ball
And love it when I score!

The weekend I can't wait for,
Saturday is *my* day,
Because if I play well that day
I get my chance to play.

Todd Lewis (7)
St Thomas Garnet's School, Bournemouth

EARTH FOR ME

Are there trees on Mercury?
No.
Has anyone on Venus seen us?
No.
Are there cars on Mars?
No.
Can I use a computer on Jupiter?
No.
Can I sit on Saturn?
No.
Does it rain on Uranus?
No.
Can I sing on Neptune?
No.
Does it snow on Pluto?
No.
Would I rather be on Earth?
Yes.

Adam Smith (7)
St Thomas Garnet's School, Bournemouth

A Walk In The Woods

I was walking through the woods one day
But I wanted someone to come and play!
I looked at the flowers; I looked at the sun
But nobody seemed to want any fun.
I thought of my friends, but where can they be?
Maybe they're hiding up in that tree.
I looked up high but there's nobody there
And then I looked down and saw my friend Claire.
I climbed down quickly to ask her to play
But when I got down she had run away!
Once again I am all alone
Perhaps now it's time for me to go home.
When I returned I suddenly saw
Somebody was standing at my door.
So that's where all my friends had been
No wonder they weren't to be seen!
Then I realised why they were there today
Of course, it was my eight birthday.

Natalie Rondeau (7)
St Thomas Garnet's School, Bournemouth

The Mermaid

See her sitting among the rocks.
Her shiny tail glittering in the sun.
See her watch boats go by, hiding between the rocks.
She swims back down to the deep, blue sea
And watches flounder go by.
Her sparkly tail changing every day,
What a beautiful thing,
The mermaid swimming down to the deep, blue sea.

Amy Pankhurst (7)
St Thomas Garnet's School, Bournemouth

The Work Machine

Once I had a machine,
It was very big and strong
And if I put my homework in
It comes out neatly done.

In the morning before school,
It gives me such a buzz
And then at school I whiz and whiz,
But one day something just went wrong.

At home I said 'What a mystery!'
But I soon found out what's up
It wasn't on, silly me
That's why it went all wrong.

So I switched it back on
And my work machine went buzzing
I shouted 'Hooray!'
My work machine will do my work again.

Kate Henman (7)
St Thomas Garnet's School, Bournemouth

Drinking Fountain

When I climb up to get a drink,
It doesn't work the way you'd think.
I turn it up, the water goes
And hits me right upon the nose!

I turn it down to make it small,
And I don't get any drink at all!

Rayna Chauhan (8)
St Thomas Garnet's School, Bournemouth

My Pony

My pony's name is Blaze,
He's very, very sweet.
He's all brown with a white blaze
And he eats my father's wheat.

His hoof is round
And very wide.
His tummy is thin
Around the side.

When he's angry,
He's not very easy to handle,
But when he's happy,
He never even bites my little brother Hansel.

When I ride him,
He bounces like a ball
And at the end of the ride,
He starts to drawl.

I love him so much,
I'll never sell him.
I won't give him to anyone,
Not even my best friend Kim.

Laura Johnson (8)
St Thomas Garnet's School, Bournemouth

The Pike

The pike moves slowly through the brown river
Hiding in the green swaying reeds
Eating every little fish he sees.
A frog is swimming on the surface
And the pike darts out, its jaws snap shut around it.

But then he sees something shiny.
Could it be another little fish?
He comes up to bite it
But it is a fisherman's hook.
He is caught.

Eoin Kerr (7)
St Thomas Garnet's School, Bournemouth

Two Thousand

It is the year two thousand,
I'm listening with my ear,
People are filling me with cheer,
And I'm beginning to see more clear.

It is near the year two thousand,
I'm listening with my ear,
People have nothing to fear,
So we're celebrating with cheer and beer.

It is near the year two thousand,
I'm listening with my ear,
We really are so happy now looking forward
To next year.

It is near the year two thousand,
I'm listening with my ear,
People are more kinder and love is in
The air.

It is near the year two thousand,
And I hope you have a healthy happy one.

Lee Fordham (9)
St Thomas Garnet's School, Bournemouth

HOCKEY

There are eleven people to a side,
Who all hit the ball long and wide.
Their aim is to defend and attack
To get lots of balls in the goal at the back.

We all play with a curved, wooden stick,
Some of us slow, some of us quick.
We stand, we run, we attack and score,
The spectators scream *'More! More!'*

Every week we meet up and say,
'Is it a match? A game? Or a practice play?'
We're out in the fresh air, stretching our legs,
Running around, doing our best.

The umpires are fair, but the games can be rough,
But we play by the rules and that can be tough.
We love to play hockey It's great fun to play,
When we score lots of goals, we all shout

Hooray!

Ben Ingram-Johnson (8)
St Thomas Garnet's School, Bournemouth

IF I WERE A PIG!

If I were a pig
I'd be a very fat pig!
I'd wallow in the mud all day.
I'd spy from my sty with my little piggy eye,
Waiting for buckets of grub to come my way!

Francesca Welsh (7)
St Thomas Garnet's School, Bournemouth

Skiing

Here I go on my skis
Through the snow and through the trees
Up the lifts
Through snow drifts
Down the hill
With a thrill
Over the ice with a crunch
Now it's time for lunch
A bowl of soup, a slice of bread,
'Back to ski school' someone said.
Over the bumps
With some jumps
One more run
Just for fun
A hot chocolate for aprés ski
Back to the hotel in time for tea.

Jamie Rickard (8)
St Thomas Garnet's School, Bournemouth

The Shire Horse

As evening draws its velvet curtain
They trudge back home through fields of mud
The day's hard labour done.
Seasons turn like pedals
And one by one the years advance
And soon their time will come.
People talk about machines that plough whole fields
In just one day, and never stop to eat or drink.
But, until then they'll carry on with tack and plough
The strain of flesh and steel, until another age.

Alice Freeman (8)
St Thomas Garnet's School, Bournemouth

ME AND MY CAT

My name is Ross
I go to school
I like to play football every day

I like to get goals
I like to get wet
Then go home and cuddle my pet

My pet is called Snowy
She's grey and white
Sometimes my sister cuddles her too tight

Snowy gets hurt but never cries
She just wriggles away and opens her eyes

I like football
I like my cat
That's all I can say
So that is that.

Ross Browne (7)
St Thomas Garnet's School, Bournemouth

LOVE

Love is one of the most
Powerful things on earth
But love can be hard sometimes
But God will love me before
My very birth
Sometimes I kick, shout and scream
And sometimes I'm good as gold
I'll try to be like Jesus
Just like He told.

Anya Kilkenny Browne (10)
St Thomas Garnet's School, Bournemouth

God Made It All

I like all the beautiful flowers,
God made them.

I like all the birds who sing,
God made them.

I like all the stars that twinkle in the sky,
God made them.

I like all the seals and the dolphins,
God made them.

God made all the things in the world,
He loves everyone and everything,

And I love Him too.

Stephen Fordham (8)
St Thomas Garnet's School, Bournemouth

Why Are They Making Such A Fuss?

Why are they making such a fuss?
It may be a millennium,
But why all the fuss?
It's 2000 years of Jesus,
But why make so much fuss?
People think if they are not there to see it, it does not happen,
So why all the fuss?
It is the millennium with 2000 years,
But why all the fuss?
Everyone is going to party at midnight,
But why oh why all the fuss?

Sean Dingley (9)
St Thomas Garnet's School, Bournemouth

The Big Match

At the football the crowds all roar and cheer,
'Come on you reds,' is the cry we all hear.
A great big win is what we want.
The whistle blows, it's kick-off time,
Let us hope we win by nine.
In the second half,
Someone has an early bath.
He pushed the ref far too hard,
So he got the old red card.
The final whistle goes at last
And the crowd give out a mighty blast.

The winners!

Patrick Fraser (7)
St Thomas Garnet's School, Bournemouth

The Save

It's cold and muddy
Wet and windy
As I stood there scared
With my knees shaking with fright

I suddenly run to the left
Then run to the right
As I see the boy's foot rise up for a strike

The ball comes towards me and hits me in the face
I fall on my tummy
I look up at the ref as he makes a sign
He blows his whistle
At last! It's full-time.

Joshua Bowman (8)
St Thomas Garnet's School, Bournemouth

Holidays

Holidays holidays
Sailing
Cold capsizing
Beaches
Hot and sunny
Adventure
Muddy hiking boots

Holidays holidays
Sightseeing
Amazing buildings
Walt Disney
Mickey and Minnie
Cruises
Exotic oceans.

Andrew Oates (10)
St Thomas Garnet's School, Bournemouth

My Car Trip

Oh no, not another trip.
I get trapped in a metal cage,
Which puts me in a right old rage.
We go bumping down the road,
Which, trust me, hurts my bum a load.
Next we go up a hill
And it really makes me feel quite ill.
Down we go right to the end
And turn round a very sharp bend.
Wait a minute, hang on a tick,
Is that my little brother being sick?

Annie Henman (9)
St Thomas Garnet's School, Bournemouth

My Ideal Dog

When I went on a walk one day
Do you know what I saw?
I saw a dog with a very big belly
Which nearly reached the floor.

His ears were floppy, his eyes were brown
His tail was wagging up and down.
His body was long, his legs were short
His bark was echoing all around.

His long pink tongue hung from one side
As he came running past,
All four paws were covered in mud
So he couldn't run very fast.

As I sat on a bench nearby
I turned and said to Dad,
'I'd love a dog like that one day'
But he replied 'No way.' How sad.

Laura Sheasby (10)
St Thomas Garnet's School, Bournemouth

The Year 2000

Our lives are going to change with all the things happening
In the year 2000.

We will see on New Year's Day amazing fireworks.
Our families will hold great partics and share presents.

Most of all we will celebrate in the year 2000
The birth of baby Jesus who came to earth all those years ago.

Anna Wazejewski (8)
St Thomas Garnet's School, Bournemouth

One Spooky Night

One spooky night,
The wolves had a fright.
When the lights went out,
I shivered all about.
When I heard the door creak,
It really made me shriek.
I stayed up all night,
From the ghostly shadow's sight.

One stormy night,
When there was no moonlight,
When I saw the lightning,
The whole sky was brightening.
Whenever it poured with rain,
I nearly went insane.
Dozing off in the night
And I dream of morning light.

Peter Michel (10)
St Thomas Garnet's School, Bournemouth

Millennium

Millennium 2000 will be our delight,
Floating cars, space rocket bars!
It will be a lovely sight.
Flying cars, they'll be high,
Very high up in the sky.
The lovely sight will be fireworks good,
Out in the open people stood.
Now the millennium will be gone,
How the fireworks, wow they shone.

Piers Bate (9)
St Thomas Garnet's School, Bournemouth

My Dog

My dog is funny when I rub his tummy and he barks at the cat. The cat just scowls back with his nose in the air and my dog seems to laugh.

Oh why is my dog so funny when I rub his tummy? I'll ask my mum. She said he's lucky because he was a rescue dog from the RSPCA and counts his blessings every day in a funny sort of way.

Birthdays and friends make my dog happy and we share in the presents and fun. A walk in the park or a stroll in the dark wood with a torch and a cake or a bun.

My dog hates rainy days, when all he does is play inside my house, with my cat and myself and my toys.

One day I will think of a name for him, so I can call him whenever I want. It must be an easy name, just like falling off a log, or perhaps it might be easier just to keep on calling him 'My Dog'!

George Soan (7)
St Thomas Garnet's School, Bournemouth

Golf

You hit the ball with a long-handled pole,
The aim of the game to putt in a hole.
Driving and putting, a hook or a slice,
It's supposed to be fun, but it's not always nice.
Start at one and end on eighteen,
The holes are apart, but there's a laugh in-between.
The fairways are long and the greens are smooth,
So long as you practice,
You're bound to improve.

James Ingram-Johnson (10)
St Thomas Garnet's School, Bournemouth

I'VE GOT A QUESTION

I've got a question, that question you should hear,
Why do people ask such silly questions?
But don't worry 'cause I won't jeer.

I've got a question, that question you should hear,
My friend and I were wondering,
Did we pass the exam or did we get them all wrong
Or did we get very, very near?

I've got a question, that question you should hear,
Why do people ask such silly questions?
But don't worry 'cause I won't jeer.

Fionnuala Craven (10)
St Thomas Garnet's School, Bournemouth

THE FANCY DRESS SHOP

Feather boas, hats and scarves,
ideas for a hundred laughs.
Jackets, coats and trousers too,
surely something here will do.
Pirates, soldiers and matadors,
are all there hidden in the stores.
So many clothes for me to choose
and then I will have to think of shoes,
I could be here for a day or more
choosing from this fantastic store.
The next party will have to be . . .
a simple occasion by the sea.

Simon Laws (10)
St Thomas Garnet's School, Bournemouth

MY BABY BROTHER

My mum,
She's great
Because
She gave me
A baby brother.
Yipee!
Born 26th January
5.52 to be exact.
That's morning by the way.
54cm long . . . already.
Nine pounds three . . . so heavy.
He's cute
He's cuddly
No teeth yet.
Oh! His name?
Harrison.
Just remember that, okay?

Sean Atkinson (9)
St Thomas Garnet's School, Bournemouth

2000

As the day draws nearer,
People are no way clearer
As to what the Millennium Bug will bring.

Everywhere all around,
Computers may shut down,
Electricity may fail
And trains go off the rail.

There might be celebration,
There might be joy,
It might be fun
For girls and boys.

So much chaos for only a date?
I wonder what will be our fate?
We'll do what we can . . .
And hope we're not late.

Oisin O'Leary (9)
St Thomas Garnet's School, Bournemouth

My World

My name is Alice
My world is real
I live with my family
Not just in fantasy
I have no white rabbit
Just a grey cat
So what would the Mad Hatter
think of that?

My mum is the Queen of Hearts
My sister bakes delicious tarts
I have family and friends
On whom I can depend

I have my health
I have my home
And look forward
To the future to come.

Alice Churchill (10)
St Thomas Garnet's School, Bournemouth

THE MILLENNIUM PARTY

Tick tock goes the clock,
We're waiting for our friends,
We're going to have a party,
We hope it never ends.

Fireworks are going off,
Look how fast they fly.
They burst and leave bright colours
Way up in the sky.
Red, yellow, green and blue,
Maybe a little violet too.

When the children hear the music playing,
They start the dance without delaying.
While the guests drink champagne,
The children they start playing games.
Up and downstairs the children flow,
Making a thumping sound as they go!

It's just past twelve, it's time for bed,
We go back up the stairs with sleepy heads.
We've welcomed in a new century,
What a wonderful future it's going to be!

Bethany Wildeman (8)
St Thomas Garnet's School, Bournemouth

MUSIC

Music is delightful,
Although some pieces are quite frightful,
Should you play the piano or guitar,
You will be heard near and far.

Flute, clarinet and trombone,
Oh such wonderful instruments!
Although each one with quite a different tone.

Those great pianists,
They play so well,
Their music seems to take you where nothing exists,
A place where angels dwell.

There's the violin with strings that are like elastic,
Music from them is fantastic.
All instruments make a beautiful sound,
Which seems to lift you off the ground.

Gareth Wilson (10)
St Thomas Garnet's School, Bournemouth

My Millennium Party

You're invited to come, New Year 2000.
Come along, we'll have some good fun!
I'm going to build a new millennium home,
With a roof that's not a dome
But a football pitch!
My millennium home won't be in Rome,
Built in space will be the place!
With 2000 lights which will light up the sky
Like 2000 angels
And parking for 2000 cars.
A robot performing 2000 tricks
To keep us entertained!
Then midnight strikes,
We'll release 2000 balloons
Like 2000 shining moons!

Rose Weston (9)
St Thomas Garnet's School, Bournemouth

A Hard Life

It's a hard life, for little me
A very hard life, as you will see

Just after dawn, with sleepy head
Those dreaded words, 'Get out of bed'

Later on, still in the nest,
'Are you still there? You little pest'

Pyjamas warm and slippers too
I shuffle off . . . into the loo

I'd like a bath, but I get a shower
Again the call 'You've half an hour!'

Fried bread with bacon and egg on top?
No, just the usual snap, crackle, pop

Into the car, it's off to school
Forgot my coat! Oh what a fool!

I have to work so hard all day
When will I get some time for play?

A nice hot lunch, a big fat steak?
Sandwiches again, give me a break!

At end of school, *now* am I free?
'Look at this homework that's been given me!'

Piano to practise and a book to read
It's watching 'The Flintstones' I *really* need

My tummy's rumbling, it's getting late
What food can I anticipate?

Some crispy chips, that juicy steak?
Not *fish* again - oh for goodness sake!

After washing up (a job I dread)
Is it time for *myself?* No . . . it's time for *bed!*

Emma Louise Tuck (10)
St Thomas Garnet's School, Bournemouth

Two Dead Men

One fine day in the middle
  Of the night,
Two dead men got
  Up to fight,
They turned around,
  Faced each other,
Drew their swords
  And shot each other.

In the morning when it
  Was dark,
The two dead men went
  To the park,
The gate was locked
  So in they went,
The swings fell down
  And the slide was bent.

Amy Stokes (11)
St Thomas Garnet's School, Bournemouth

My Beanie Bear

I thought I would write this poem
To tell you about my favourite bear,
He's lovely and cuddly and cute,
With beautiful soft, brown hair.

I take him to bed with me every night,
He keeps me safe and warm,
So I snuggle up and hold him tight,
Then neither of us will come to any harm.

I love his big, black, shining eyes,
And his body full of beans,
So I'm sure it comes as no surprise,
To know that he means the world to me.

Laura Marie Gillings (10)
St Thomas Garnet's School, Bournemouth

Millennium

At the millennium we shall be celebrating 2000 years of
the birth of Jesus Christ in a stable in Bethlehem.
If he were here today, what would He think of the world?
Motor cars
Computers
Aeroplanes
Television
Medicines
Space travel
Modern houses
Electricity
Mobile phones
Wouldn't He be surprised!

Lucy Trapp (9)
St Thomas Garnet's School, Bournemouth

THE PHANTOM GHOST

The phantom's mask speaks words of ghost,
His cape will hide his face,
But yet none of us will ever know
Who's the phantom ghost.
Backstage in the bleak
We will never hear him speak.
But through the darkness we will seek
To find the phantom ghost.
He will never see the dawn,
Or the birds fly high.
We will only hear his groan,
And his faithful sigh.
But one mystery that remains that hasn't been at host,
What we all would like to know is . . .
Who's the phantom ghost?

Sian Lister (9)
Sandford St Martin's First School

THE FALCON

Once on a high cliff stood a proud falcon,
It zooms in like a torpedo in water.
Why does he zoom so fast like a bullet in brass?
It would stand there all day until nightfall,
Where it lay until the break of day.
He would stand so far where people would think he was a star.
How long will he stand there up so high?
Until he is ready to die.

Jonathan Belfield (8)
Sandford St Martin's First School

The Silver Stars And Moons

Silver is the moon
Silver are the stars
Silver is the galaxy
With Pluto, Jupiter and Mars
Your love can shine
Like heavens above
The doves fly
But I can die
Of the silver moon and the silver stars.

Jessica Evans (9)
Sandford St Martin's First School

Tormented

Tormented just because of the colour of their skin,
Why can't people see the true person within.
Spite, hate, vandalism, driven into taking drugs,
They were nice when they started off, though they've been transformed
To thugs,
Tiny little quarrel, turns into a big fight,
Air-raid sirens, bombing, terror through the night.
Babies and young children hide under their beds,
Teenagers weeping, crying, wishing they were dead.
Why can't this generation live in peace and harmony?
We only care about ourselves, well that and our money,
Why can't we hold out our bare hand instead of a loaded gun,
When there's a nuclear war, we'll be disgraced by what we've done.
So please try to be friendly or to our utter dismay,
They'll be no happiness in the world
And the Earth will fade away.

Lauren Downes (11)
Upton Junior School

Birds

Happy birds,
Flying high,
Whizzing right across the sky.
Happy birds,
Making nests
With feathers from their fluffy crests.

Frightened birds,
Victims of dogs,
Killed and sold and cooked with hogs.
Frightened birds,
Flying away,
From men with guns, towards the sun's ray.

Liberty Smith (10)
Upton Junior School

Flowers

Red poppies, yellow daffodils,
Why do we try and destroy them?
Sunflowers, black spots with great yellow frills,
Why do we try and destroy them?
We gaze at them, smell them, then pick for gifts,
Some lovely flowers give beautiful wiffs.
The world looks so much more beautiful
With flowers and trees,
So why do we try and destroy them?

Clemency Bunn (11)
Upton Junior School

OUR WORLD TODAY

The air is full of fumes,
The sea is full of oil,
The rain has turned to acid
And the rivers are full of waste.
This wouldn't be so bad, if there was
Nothing we could do,
But we can,
We can and it's up to you.

Cut down on using cars,
Recycle all our waste,
Ban nuclear energy
And tidy up the place.

So now we know what we can do,
You'd better get to work,
You know if we don't save the earth,
It will only get worse.

We don't want the air full of fumes,
The sea full of oil,
The rain turning to acid
And rivers full of waste.

Charlotte Davis (11)
Upton Junior School

WHAT A DISGRACE!

Poachers, all around the world,
Killing for their own good.
Whales, for eating,
For people at meetings.
What a disgrace!
Gorillas, kept in a zoo,
Just to entertain me and you.
What a disgrace!
Tigers, killed for clothes,
Just so we can pose.
What a disgrace!
Dolphins, caught for training,
We just think *how entertaining!*
What a disgrace!
Stop, stop, stop all this
Before the animal world is nothing
But missed.

What a disgrace!

Francesca Gumbs (11)
Upton Junior School